the
anxiety, worry
& depression
workbook

65 exercises, worksheets & tips to improve mood and feel better

Jennifer L. Abel, PhD

"This workbook is a valuable resource for managing anxiety, worry and depression. If you are personally looking for help or are a professional who treats people with these conditions, you have here a treasure trove of ideas. Dr. Abel's worksheets will guide you through the process to shake off depressing anxiety and worry, and then walk you into a more positive life."

-**Margaret Wehrenberg, PsyD,**
Author of *The 10 Best-Ever Anxiety Management Techniques* and
Anxiety + Depression: Effective Treatment of the Big Two Co-Occurring Disorders

"Anxiety and depression often go hand in hand, and worry is common experience across both problems. This is the first book that I know of to focus on the role of worry in both anxiety and depression. The book is filled with practical strategies that are quick and straightforward. The easy-to-use worksheets and bonus downloadable recordings make this especially useful for anyone struggling with anxiety and depression, as well as their therapists!"

-**Martin M. Antony, PhD,**
Professor of Psychology, Ryerson University
Author of the *Shyness and Social Anxiety Workbook* and *The Anti-Anxiety Workbook*

The Anxiety, Worry & Depression Workbook
Copyright © 2018 by Jennifer L. Abel

Published by
PESI Publishing & Media
PESI, Inc
3839 White Ave
Eau Claire, WI 54703

Cover: Amy Rubenzer
Editing: Hazel Bird
Layout: Amy Rubenzer & Bookmasters

ISBN: 9781683731092

Printed in the United States of America.

PESI
Publishing
& Media
www.pesi.com

About the Author

Jennifer L. Abel, PhD, international speaker, author and clinical psychologist, has specialized in the treatment of anxiety disorders for over 25 years. Before opening a private practice, she served as the associate director of the Stress and Anxiety Disorders Institute at Penn State under the direction of the leading expert in Generalized Anxiety Disorder (GAD), T.D. Borkovec.

She is the author of the bestselling card deck, *Melt Worry & Relax Card Deck: 56 CBT & Mindfulness Strategies to Release Anxiety*. Her first book, *Active Relaxation,* has received outstanding reviews from mental health care professionals and anxious readers alike. Her second book, *Resistant Anxiety, Worry, and Panic*, has received praise from top experts in anxiety management.

Dr. Abel has published many articles in professional journals and wrote a pamphlet about GAD for ABCT. She has been quoted by several popular magazines (e.g., *Health, Prevention, Glamour*) for her expertise in worry. Dr. Abel presents to the public (e.g., *Working Women's Survival Show*), as well as professionals (e.g., *Australian Psychological Society; PESI Inc.*).

Table of Contents

Introduction

As a clinical psychologist, I have specialized in treating anxiety since my graduate school practicum at Chestnut Ridge Hospital in 1989. During my post-doctoral work at Penn State's Stress and Anxiety Disorders Institute, under the direction of T.D. Borkovec, I focused my expertise on generalized anxiety disorder (GAD); and after almost 10 years of research, I started a private practice. As a scientist-practitioner, I always consider, and use, strategies for anxiety and depression that have been proven to work in scientific, clinical studies. However, there is also an art to being a great clinician. Taking into consideration both art and science, I have created several unique strategies, and modified mainstream approaches, to effectively help thousands of individuals struggling with anxiety, worry, and depression through my direct clinical work, and also by teaching thousands of clinicians through my seminars, my book, and my therapy cards. Because of the uniqueness of my strategies, many of the ones found in these exercises and worksheets are not found in any other self-help books or workbooks.

WHY THIS BOOK IS UNIQUE

There are countless books on the topics of depression, worry, and anxiety. However, this is the first book that addresses the relationship between worry and depression, as well as the anxiety caused by worry. I chose a workbook format and included recordings because we learn better when we experience information in a variety of ways. This workbook will help you change your habits through reading, writing, listening, and engaging in several experiments. I've also included self-monitoring forms, because when you keep track of the concepts in the book, it increases the likelihood you will continue to use these strategies on a daily basis, which in turn greatly increases the likelihood of success.

Worry is typically thought to cause anxiety; however, it causes a significant amount of depression (Andrews & Borkovec, 1988). In fact, people with GAD are more likely to develop depression or dysthymia (a chronic low-level depression) than those whose worry and anxiety is healthy. We also know that when we treat worry, even with only relaxation and mindfulness strategies, depression lifts (Borkovec, Abel, & Newman, 1995). Likewise, early in my career I treated many people whose primary concern was depression, only to learn that worry was driving a significant amount of their depression. Typically, these individuals didn't mention that they worried a lot, as they had grown almost accustomed to their worry and often considered it a trait that they couldn't change. Once we addressed the worry, the depression lifted.

Not only is the relationship between worry and depression not known to the public, it's not common knowledge amongst mental health care professionals. Furthermore, most health care professionals aren't experienced in using the strategies most effective for worry. Therefore, the second half of the workbook is a guide specifically for therapists. If you're currently working with a therapist, they can use this section to better inform and complement the exercises in the first half of the workbook. If you don't see a therapist, you might consider seeing one who specializes in cognitive-behavioral therapy (CBT) or dialectical-behavioral therapy (DBT).

HOW TO USE THIS BOOK

Many books are read, but not consumed. You can get more out of one self-help book that you apply to your life than by reading a dozen.

This book has two parts, a self-help workbook for those dealing with depression, worry and anxiety, as well as a therapists' guide at the end. The workbook format of this book provides encouragement to make it easier for you to process the information and apply the strategies. For the best results, read one chapter at a time and apply the strategies in that chapter for a week, perhaps longer, before moving on to the next chapter. It is important not to rush through things; it is only as you take time to apply these strategies that you will receive the most benefit from them. Be sure to also engage in the experiments and to listen to the recordings. Keep in mind that some strategies and experiments will work better for you than others—one of the reasons that multiple techniques are provided.

It is recommended that you use this book with your therapist, who will ideally own this book as well. They can help to guide you through the chapters that will be most beneficial for you, and may change the order to best help you. However, due to constraints like time, money, travel or living in a remote area, you may also choose to try the workbook on your own.

If you are anxious, or you are depressed and worry, Chapters 1-17 address these topics and will likely be beneficial for you. Chapters 18-23 address issues that people with depression or anxiety may or may not deal with. There are questions at the beginning of each of these last chapters to help you determine if the issue applies to you. Feel free to skip any of these chapters that are not relevant to you.

Utilize the free recordings recommended in this workbook by going to AnxietyStLouisPsychologist.com/free.

On this website, you will see two black boxes reading **Free Mindfulness Recordings** and **Free Walking Mindfulness Recording**. Click on these to download the first five recordings referenced in this workbook. Track 4 in the free recordings, entitled "General Mindfulness," can be used for quiet relaxation; additional quiet relaxation recordings are available for purchase for only $4.99. These optional recordings may be purchased from the same page. The guide to these recordings is available online; however, for your convenience, a description of all the recordings is listed below along with the accompanying chapter:

1. Observing Emotion (Chapter 3) – This track is to be used when experiencing uncomfortable emotions. Remember while using this track that some emotions are healthy. The goal is to accept emotions without adding to their discomfort by trying to fight them. When successful, unhealthy emotions subside.

2. Observing Thoughts (Chapter 4) – This track should be used when worrying. When mindful and accepting of thoughts, unhealthy thoughts tend to decrease or subside completely.

3. Labeling Thoughts (Chapter 4) – When observing and accepting thoughts doesn't work, we often feel the futility of our thoughts in a whole new way by simply attaching labels to them.

4. General Mindfulness (Chapter 7) – This track can be used while sitting quietly, lying down with your eyes closed, or while doing any activity.

5. Walking Mindfulness (Chapter 7) – Use this recording with one earbud out, while on a walk or a run.

There are two types of quiet relaxation tracks. The first three involve imagery to use when you are having difficulty getting rid of troublesome thoughts or worries. The second set is true quiet relaxation that may be used after the imagery tracks or alone.

Imagery to help quiet the mind:

1. Balloons (Chapter 12) – This track is most useful when you have many things "on your plate" and you're having difficulty concentrating on a task or are unable to enjoy leisurely activity.

2. Sink (Chapter 12) – This track can be used whether you have one thing on your mind or many things on your mind.

3. Record Player (Chapter 12) – This track is the most helpful when your thoughts are spinning out of control.

Quiet relaxation:

4. Ocean (Chapter 12) –If you're using earbuds or headphones, keep one earbud out.

5. Sponge (Chapter 12) – This track is most useful when you're experiencing muscle tension.

6. Clouds (Chapter 12) – This track is also helpful for reducing muscle tension. However, it is generally very relaxing, even if you have no issues with muscle tension.

7. Breathing (Chapter 12) – This track offers a variety of ideas to use in conjunction with focusing on your breathing.

8. All Senses Mindfulness (Chapter 7) – Before listening to this track, gather the following things: a) candles, incense, or both; b) a beverage – preferably a warm aromatic beverage or a small amount of wine; c) a piece of chocolate (other finger foods will suffice, but avoid anything crunchy or chewy). Light the incense and/or candles and consider placing them in front of a window, pleasant art work, or a blank wall across from somewhere that you can sit comfortably.

9. All Senses Less Sound (Chapter 7) – This is the same track as the previous track, with the volume of the nature sounds reduced.

10. Nature Sounds Alone (Chapter 7) – This track has only the nature sounds, should you wish to guide yourself on the remaining senses.

If you do not wish to access these recordings, there are scripts in the chapters that you may use instead.

HOW THERAPISTS CAN USE THIS WORKBOOK

It is recommended that you read the client portion of the workbook along with the accompanying chapter of the therapists' guide before using this workbook with clients. Consider using the workbook portion for yourself, particularly if the chapter applies to you—even if only to a subclinical extent. Remember, however, that responses to the strategies vary, so if something works for you, don't necessarily assume it will work for your client; and if a strategy doesn't help you, it may still be very effective with your client.

Except in rare cases, even clients whose primary complaint is depression will benefit from the chapters addressing worry and anxiety, since worry often contributes significantly to depression. In addition, many of the chapters directly address both depression and anxiety.

Likewise, all the chapters that address depression are likely to be helpful for those who don't suffer from depression, except Chapter 17: Getting Motivated to Manage Depression. Motivated clients who suffer from depression will not need this chapter.

While I encourage you to skip around the book, matching the chapters with clients' symptoms and presentation, it is best to start by reading the first two chapters. Chapters 18-23 certainly will not apply to everyone, and it is unlikely that all five of these chapters will apply to any one individual.

For best results:

1. If possible, engage clients in the experiments before they read the content in the chapters.

2. Encourage your client to share and discuss their worksheets with you. Make blank copies for them; it will improve adherence.

3. Ask your clients to practice the strategies in each chapter for at least a few days—preferably a week or more—before moving on to the next concept.

4. Encourage your clients to use the self-monitoring forms. Compliance is more likely if you provide copies and ask them to bring the completed forms each session. Reviewing and discussing them at each session will improve adherence.

5. Either encourage your clients to download the recordings, or make the recordings for them yourself. (See Chapter 12 of the Therapists' Guide, p. 149.)

Best wishes for increasing your own well-being and to more relaxed and happier clients!

Part 1

Anxiety, Worry, & Depression
Workbook

1 | Worry:
Chapter

The Root of Anxiety and Depression

Nearly everyone worries at least occasionally. About one in four people believe that they worry too much. While worry is usually thought to cause anxiety, it often leads to depression too. Whether we're worried or not, negative thinking usually leads to anxiety, depression, and sometimes other uncomfortable emotions such as embarrassment, guilt, and frustration. When anxiety interferes with the enjoyment of life, it can cause depression too. There are a number of other issues that can lead to depression and anxiety, such as hormone imbalances, genetics, side-effects of medication, and disease. While there appears to be a small genetic influence, worry is primarily a habit that is learned. People tend to "get used to" their worry habits and often don't realize how much those habits are affecting their mental and physical health.

Worry can be defined as thoughts or images that lead to anxiety or prevent relaxation and that are not productive. Planning and problem-solving involve productive thinking that may include some level of pressure or anxiety, but it's not necessary. Worries are typically useless thoughts that tend to be repetitive. Not only is it not productive, but worry has also been proven to interfere with problem-solving.

People who worry excessively and meet criteria for a disorder known as generalized anxiety disorder not only experience more anxiety and depression than others but are also more prone to many medical problems, including heart disease, headaches, and irritable bowel syndrome. Worry also puts you at risk for major depressive disorder, dysthymia (mild chronic depression), and other anxiety disorders that are often more severe, such as panic disorder, phobias, and obsessive–compulsive disorder.

When we experience threat, our bodies gear us up to fight and run, so we can protect ourselves from harm. Sometimes anxiety is healthy in that it may help us to literally run or fight to survive. Other times, the anxiety may motivate us to get out of a bad situation, such as an unhealthy relationship or a toxic job. However, worry and anxiety that do not motivate us to protect ourselves are false alarms to the body. Our bodies react the same way to worry as they do to actual threat, but with nothing to fight and nowhere to run. This explains the connection between worry and medical problems as well as some of the uncomfortable symptoms that accompany worry, such as muscle tension.

Unfortunately, modern medicine often treats the symptoms of a problem rather than the cause. In this case, worried habits, negative thinking, and several other unhealthy habits are usually the cause of anxiety, depression, and medical problems, and patients are often medicated instead of being encouraged to change their habits. Worry, as the seed of so many mental health and medical problems, is usually overlooked, and seldom do physicians recommend to their patients that they see a cognitive–behavioral therapist to treat their worry.

Do You Have Generalized Anxiety Disorder?

1. Do you believe that your worry is uncontrollable? _____

2. Check the symptoms below that you experience at least sometimes:

❑ Difficulty concentrating

❑ Fatigue

❑ Insomnia

❑ Irritability

❑ Muscle tension

❑ Feeling keyed up, on edge, or nervous

Now circle the symptoms above that you experience more days than not.

Did you check at least three symptoms, circle at least two, and say yes to the first question?

If so, and if you have been bothered by these symptoms for at least six months, you probably have generalized anxiety disorder. If all the symptoms applied but you have had them for less than six months, you are probably just going through an adjustment period that could either resolve with time or lead to generalized anxiety disorder.

Often people develop generalized anxiety disorder in childhood or adolescence. However, it can start with a major life event, such as going to graduate school, having children, divorce, losing a loved one, or retirement. The good news is that treatment for generalized anxiety disorder is usually very effective without using medication (e.g., Borkovec, Newman, Pincus, & Lytle, 2002). Furthermore, when worry lifts, mood and health improve as well. There are two very important things to understand about the nature of worry and anxiety to begin to heal and form more relaxing and healthy habits. The first is that anxiety occurs in a spiral of interactions between thoughts, images, physical sensations, behaviors, and emotions. Waiting too long to intervene with coping strategies will usually render those strategies useless. The second important aspect of the nature of worry is that fighting it fuels it. **Many of the exercises and worksheets to come include ways to circumvent and even do the opposite of fighting it: surrender to or accept it.**

It is recommended that you work with a therapist who is well-trained in using cognitive–behavioral therapy and either mindfulness or dialectic behavioral therapy. However, using this workbook without the help of a therapist can be very helpful. One option is to use the workbook and, if you aren't happy with the results, see a therapist later.

Self-monitoring is a useful tool, as it has been proven to improve results. Some of the worksheets include self-monitoring, to help increase the likelihood that you will follow through on the advice. It will also help you to track your progress. I suggest that you use the simple monitoring form found on the next page at the end of each day.

Daily Self-Monitoring

Rate each emotion on a 0–10 scale with a 10 being the most anxious, depressed, or irritable you have ever been and 0 being completely relaxed, very happy, and not at all irritated. If one or two of the emotions aren't problematic, feel free to skip rating them. For "Applying Strategies," you can give yourself a grade (e.g., B+), or rate yourself on a 0–10.

Date	Anxiety	Depression	Irritability	Applying Strategies?
11/1	7	2	5	C

2 Chapter | Fighting Worry and Anxiety Fuels It

| EXERCISE | Blue Monkeys |

Think about blue monkeys. Now stop thinking about blue monkeys. Put the book down for about 30 seconds.

What have you been thinking about? If you are like most people, you thought about blue monkeys. In the space below, write down what you've been worried about.

_____

_____

_____

_____

_____

_____

Now, stop worrying about that. Put it out of your mind. Again, put down the book for about 30 seconds.

If you're like most people, you are now worrying about the topic I asked you to put out of your mind and the intensity of your thoughts is greater than with the monkeys. Daniel Wegner (1989) showed people a picture of a white bear and told half of them not to think about the white bear. People told not to think about the bear were much more likely to be thinking about the bear 10 minutes later. After the white bear research, Wegner did a similar experiment with worries. When people were told not to worry about something they had been worrying about, of course, they worried about it more than those who were simply asked what they worried about. Furthermore, the effect with the worry was much greater than with the neutral white bear. And what is it that others tell us when we're worried? What is it that we tell ourselves when we are worried? "Don't think about it," or "Put it out of your mind."

If trying to put it out of your mind doesn't work, what does? Fortunately, there are several coping strategies that are helpful. For example, the opposite of trying to put it out of your mind is helpful. This means accepting the worry and accepting the physical sensation of anxiety, sadness, and anger. However, keep in mind that some emotion is healthy, such as crying when your pet dies or feeling anxious when there is actual threat. When emotions are healthy, it's best to do the same thing—accept them—but expect that when they are healthy, you'll continue to feel them (for more on healthy emotion, see Chapter 11). Other things to do instead of fighting anxiety include using process words, moving toward relaxation rather than fighting anxiety, problem-solving, cognitive therapy, and postponing worry. All of these concepts will be introduced in later chapters of this book.

There are a number of audio tracks for use with this book. There are two groups of tracks. One group is free and the other group is optional and can be purchased for a small fee ($4.99). The book contains scripts if you prefer to use them in lieu of the free recordings. Most of the recordings that are available for purchase also have scripts. Some of the scripts do not match the recordings but are similar. The first script is found in the next chapter.

If you wish to use the scripts as a template to make your own recordings, see Chapter 12 of the Therapists' Guide, Relaxation & Making Recordings, for information on how to do this. **The link for both sets of recordings is AnxietyStLouisPsychologist.com/free.**

3
Chapter | Mindfulness of Physical Sensation and Emotion

In Chapter 2, you experienced that fighting unwanted thoughts fuels them. The same is true of emotions. When we fight unwanted emotions, it typically makes us feel worse. Just observing our emotions often actually lessens them.

EXERCISE Observing Feelings

If you are feeling anxious, depressed, frustrated, or other uncomfortable emotions, read the following script. (If you aren't feeling uncomfortable now, fold down the corner of this page or put a page marker here so you can come back to it when you are anxious or otherwise distressed):

Observing where you feel discomfort. Noticing where it is located in your body [pause]. Noticing how it feels [pause]. Observing how much space it takes up [pause]. Thinking about what color it would be if you could see it [pause]. What texture would it be if you could feel it? Visualizing your discomfort with color and texture.

Reread this script and then simulate what you remember with your eyes closed.

What did you notice from doing this exercise?

_____

_____

_____

_____

Were you able to just observe your emotion? Or did you find yourself trying to fight the discomfort?

_____

_____

_____

_____

Sometimes just observing how we feel is helpful. Noticing how the discomfort feels instead of fighting it will often relieve it. Sometimes observing feelings is easier than thinking of accepting them. However, the ultimate goal in the treatment of worry, anxiety, frustration, and all emotion is to accept the feelings. Part of this is surrendering by avoiding fighting the anxiety. In the next exercise, you can listen to the free recording "Observing Emotion." The recording combines observation of physical sensations from the previous script with acceptance from the Accepting Emotions exercise in the script below. Alternatively, read the following script now or at a time in the future when you are struggling with unhealthy emotions:

EXERCISE Accepting Emotions

Observing your emotion. Noticing where it's located in your body and how it feels. Letting go of any efforts to try to change it, but if it changes allowing it to change [pause]. If it increases, allowing it to increase [pause]. If it decreases, allowing it to decrease [pause]. Doing the opposite of trying to change it [pause]. Don't try to push it away and don't try to make it stay. Giving up any struggle. Just observing it as if you're an outsider looking in. Even though it's uncomfortable, accepting it.

What did you notice? Did this help more or less than the previous script? Or did the recording help more than the scripts?

_____

_____

_____

_____

Did you find yourself resisting your anxiety (or whatever your targeted emotion was)?

_____

_____

_____

_____

If these scripts and recording were not helpful for you, you may find metaphors resonate in a way that will help the concept "click" for you. In all the following metaphors, like with emotions, the more you fight the problem, the more you fuel it. Your therapist may have more metaphors, but here are some favorites:

Devil's Snare from Harry Potter

Whether you're a fan of the Harry Potter franchise or not, the devil's snare plant in *Harry Potter and the Sorcerer's Stone* (film released in 2001) is a great metaphor for acceptance. The young wizards get caught up in a root system in which the more they struggle to get free, the tighter the roots wrap around them. The roots can squeeze so tightly that they can even kill you! Hermione urges the boys to stop fighting and relax. When she and Harry surrender, they are quickly released as the roots loosen. Ron desperately struggles to free himself, causing the roots to squeeze him more tightly. Not familiar with it? Search for "devil's snare" on YouTube.

Antagonistic Sibling

Your brother is antagonizing you. If you tell him to stop it, whine, or tell your mom, it will only fuel him. The more he sees that he's upsetting you, the more he is fueled to keep doing it. If you pretend that what he's doing doesn't bother you, he will probably stop. Even consider taking it a step further: tell him to keep doing it, tell him you like it, or agree with his taunting (e.g., "You're right, I am a dork"). Then he will stop.

Bees

Swat at bees and they will be more likely to swarm and sting. Surrender and they will be likely to settle and less likely to sting.

These are all metaphors for illustrating the phenomenon that fighting anxiety fuels it. Like the devil's snare, antagonistic siblings, and bees, anxiety gets worse when you fight it and eases—sometimes even stops—when you stop fighting and accept it.

Finally, we can take this one step further: paradoxical intent. **Sometimes going a step *beyond* acceptance helps us more than just acceptance.** The idea here is to think of being brave and facing the uncomfortable symptoms head on. Usually when you're faced with a bully, if you put your hands behind your back and tell them to go ahead and take their best shot, they walk away. Anxiety is often the same way. If your heart is racing, tell it to speed up and go faster. If your chest is tight, tell it to get even tighter. If you feel shaky, think "shake harder." This can also work for crying, particularly if you feel your crying is an overreaction. If you cry about the fact that you're crying and give yourself permission to cry by trying to cry harder, the crying usually decreases or stops!

However, remember that crying is often a healthy response to sad life events or excessive frustration. See Chapter 11 for more on this.

If, after observing your anxiety and being guided to accept your anxiety, you are still fighting the anxiety, revisit the recordings or scripts, or look again at the metaphors if you felt they were helpful.

4 | Mindfulness of Thought

Chapter

Our thoughts are often the source of our uncomfortable feelings. When troublesome thoughts decrease, our bodies relax and we feel less anxious and less depressed. Also, as in the previous chapter, when our bodies relax, our thoughts can relax too. In addition, we problem-solve better and are more likely to believe positive thoughts. Like our emotions, we can both observe and accept our thoughts, instead of fighting them. More than likely you have heard about the positive qualities of mindfulness. It is a mental state in which you are aware of thoughts, senses, actions, or motivations. Without always recognizing it, you probably engage in mindful activities every day even if only for a few seconds. While mindfulness has been a way of life for many centuries in Eastern culture and essential to the path of enlightenment, it has only recently become commonplace in the Western world. Jon Kabat-Zinn (1990) is often credited with integrating Mindfulness into Western society.

EXERCISE Observing Thoughts

Read the following script or listen to the second free recording, "Observing Thoughts."

Purposefully begin to think about something that you have been worried about and that you have wanted to stop thinking about [pause]. Observing the thoughts that are going on in your mind [pause]. From here on out, don't try to think and don't try to not think. Instead, be a passive observer by just noticing the thoughts that are going on in your mind without judgment [pause]. You may be inclined to try to think or you may be inclined to try to put the thoughts out of your mind. Do neither. Letting go of all effort except to just observe and accept any thoughts that go through your mind. Observing these thoughts almost as if you're an outsider looking in, almost as if you're watching cars pass by or birds flying by.

What was your experience?

_____

_____

_____

_____

Were you trying *not* to think? If so, consider the metaphors in the previous chapter, ask your therapist for more metaphors, or read the therapists' guide for more metaphors. Then reread the script, remember the essence of it, and observe and accept your thoughts accordingly. Give it time. Consider setting a timer for a minute. If this didn't ease your thoughts, the next exercise probably will.

Every thought that we have is either a new thought or a repeat thought. Repeat thoughts are thoughts that we've had before and new thoughts are thoughts that we have for the first time. While every worry is a new thought once, most worried thoughts are repeat thoughts because we think of them several times before we put them to rest.

If just observing your thoughts automatically frees you of unwanted thoughts, there is no need for you to go to the next exercise at this moment. However, you may find it helpful in the future if observation and acceptance alone are of limited effectiveness. Listen to the free recording "Labeling Thoughts" or read the next exercise. When using the script, it's best to read it first, remember the essence of the instructions, close your eyes, and then apply it.

EXERCISE   Mindful Labeling of Thoughts

Label each thought that you have as being either "new" or "repeat": "repeat" if you've ever had the thought before, "new" if it's a new or unique thought. If you're not certain, don't get stuck on deciding; rather label it "new" or "pass." If you're alone, label aloud. Purposefully bring up something you've been worried about [pause]. Once you begin worrying, just observe the thoughts as if you're an outsider looking in [pause]. After each thought, label the thought as being "new" or "repeat" starting now. Do this for at least a minute or until your mind feels settled.

What did you experience?

_____

_____

_____

_____

_____

The hope is that you felt the futility of your repetitive thoughts in a new way. You've known for some time that your worried thoughts are excessive, useless, and burdensome. When people label each thought as being a "new" or a "repeat" thought, they usually decrease or stop completely within a minute! Sometimes other labels of thoughts are more helpful. Beneath are a few other options. Circle the ones you'd like to try. And consider adding your own labels.

• Helpful, Not Helpful, Neutral

Positive thoughts or problem-solving ideas are helpful, worries are not helpful, and neutral thoughts are neither—e.g., "I'm hungry." Similarly:

• Useful, Useless (or Not Useful), Neutral   • Worry, Other

• Wanted, Unwanted   • Past, Present, Future

• Useful, Silly, Neutral

Next time you practice either mindful acceptance or mindful labeling of your thoughts, you can follow it with a relaxation strategy.

In addition to labeling our thoughts, we can label our emotions. Chapter 11 highlights healthy emotions. When emotions are healthy, we want to accept them. When emotions are not healthy, they are useless and detrimental. Sometimes our emotions are completely healthy, sometimes they are completely unhealthy, and sometimes they are a mix of the two.

Use the following exercise any time you are uncomfortable with your emotions. The hope is that unhealthy emotions will release while healthy emotions persist.

EXERCISE   Labeling Emotion

Next time you feel an unwanted emotion or discomfort in your body, whether it's a pit in your stomach, a lump in your throat, heaviness in your chest, or something else, try labeling that feeling as "useful" or "useless," or instead "helpful" or "not helpful." Labeling it as "wanted" and "unwanted" can also be helpful.

End with a relaxation or mindfulness exercise.

Self-Monitoring of Observation and Acceptance

We tend to use coping strategies and develop habits more consistently when we self-monitor. The following will help you to keep track of mindful observation and acceptance practices more consistently. Complete this simple monitoring form daily. Under "% of Time Worrying," place your guess of the percentage of time you spent worrying; a range is okay. Under "% of Time Feeling Unhealthy Emotions," place your guess of the percentage of time you felt uncomfortable when it wasn't a healthy response to your situation; a range is okay. Under the remaining categories write one of the following:

Y = did most of the time
N = forgot to do or chose not to do
ST = sometimes; did at least once
NA = not needed (no worries or unwanted emotions, or they were fleeting)

Date	% of Time Worrying	% of Time Feeling Unhealthy Emotions	Observed Thoughts	Labeled Thoughts	Observed Emotions	Labeled Emotions
11/1	70-80%	60%	ST	N	ST	Y

Another way of being mindful of thought is by noticing that what we think affects how we feel. The words we use when we attempt to alleviate tension and anxiety are often words that mean we're fighting anxiety; therefore, sometimes they have the opposite of the calming effect we intend. A very simple and small change in the words we use can make a big difference in the way we feel and the effectiveness of the strategies we use.

EXERCISE   Command, Process or State?

1. Notice where you feel anxiety in your body now. If you don't feel much at the moment, think about where you feel it in your body when you feel anxious or worried.

2. Focus on that place or places now.

3. Remember these three words:

   Relax, Relaxing, Relaxed

4. Soon, I'm going to ask you to close your eyes and say each of these three words aloud (or in your mind if you are in a public place). Pause in between each word while noticing how you feel.

5. Then repeat each of the words in reverse order, continuing to notice how you feel.

6. When you're ready, close your eyes and begin.

7. Which word felt the best? _____

If you are like most people, you didn't pick "relax." Has anyone ever told you to relax and you've found you just want to flip 'em off? Or it just makes you less relaxed? That's because "relax" is a command. Commands create tension and even anxiety. When trying hard to relax or let go unsuccessfully time after time, many people feel hopeless and depressed. Like when we try not to think about blue monkeys (see Chapter 2), when we try too hard to resist our anxiety, at best, it isn't helpful and it usually leaves us frustrated or more anxious. Command words make us try harder than process words do.

"Relaxing" is a process word. Unlike commands, process words do not create tension. It's more natural too, because becoming relaxed is not immediate—it *is* a process. Nothing in nature goes from high to low or fast to stop in an instant. Therefore, process words are much more comfortable. Relaxed is a state of being. It is also not a command, so it is more likely to be helpful than "relax." If you picked "relax," it may have only been because it was first in the list, and it may also only have been the most helpful to you because it was first. So choose either "Relaxing" or "Relaxed" for the next exercise.

Note: Throughout this book, you may notice the use of process words even when they are grammatically incorrect.

Finding Your Most Relaxing Words

If you chose "Relaxing," use the left-hand column. If you chose "Relaxed," use the list on the right.

1. Focusing on the places in your body where you typically feel anxiety.

2. Closing your eyes, say the words below with a pause after each one, noticing which feels best. Then, check the box of the word that felt best to you.

   ❑ Calming   ❑ Calm
   ❑ Softening   ❑ Soft
   ❑ Releasing   ❑ Released

3. Repeat the above instructions with the next two sets of words below.

   ❑ Loosening   ❑ Loose
   ❑ Letting go   ❑ Peaceful
   ❑ Chillin'   ❑ Chill (as "I am chill," not "Chill out")

   ❑ Breathing   ❑ Light
   ❑ Freeing   ❑ Free
   ❑ Settling   ❑ Tranquil

4. Below write the three words you checked above. If you'd like, you can add "Relaxing" or "Relaxed" to the list. Alternatively, you can add a word or two of your own.

   ❑ _____
   ❑ _____
   ❑ _____
   ❑ _____

5. Read the list above while noticing how you feel. Narrow your favorites down to two or three. Next, close your eyes and think or say those two to three. Check the best one. You may check more than one if you'd like.

6. In the days to come, instead of telling yourself to relax, chill out, calm down, or breathe, use the word or words above when you feel anxious or tense. If you chose states of being (e.g., loose, tranquil) these words *might* be of limited effectiveness while you are anxious or frustrated. If they aren't effective, it may be that they aren't believable. For example, if you are very anxious, "loose" may seem so incongruent with how you feel that it doesn't work. Process words may work best in this situation. So, when you are feeling anxious, if the state-of-being word that you chose isn't working, experiment with the equivalent process word instead (e.g., "loosening" instead of "loose"; "becoming tranquil" instead of "tranquil").

7. Share this idea with the people who are closest to you, particularly if you find them using command words to try to help you. Encourage them to use process words when they notice that you are worried, anxious, or frustrated. When others use commands, translate them into states of being or process words in your mind. So, if someone tells you to "let it go," think in your mind "letting go."

5 Chapter | Don't Worry, Problem-Solve

At least one of the reasons you worry is that you want to have control of your life. You are trying to increase the likelihood that things will turn out well and decrease the likelihood that things will turn out poorly. You might erroneously believe that if you don't worry, things will turn out poorly. If you believe that worry has some type of protective effect on you and your loved ones, certainly check out Chapter 20, on superstitious worry. If instead, you believe that worrying will help you to make better decisions, think again. The reality is that research indicates that worry actually interferes with problem-solving. Anxiety and worried habits have a way of putting blinders on, such that solutions are less likely to come to mind. Almost certainly, you have experienced times when you stopped worrying about something, began to relax, and then voilà, a solution popped into your mind.

Some worries aren't amenable to problem-solving, but many are. One very simple approach to managing worry is to think about what you can do about it and whether you believe any of those things are worth putting into action. If there is nothing you can or want to do about your worry, it is completely useless. Basically, there are three things you can do with a worry: do something, do nothing, or plan to do something later (or plan to do something if and when it is needed).

EXERCISE Allowing Helpful Ideas to Arise

1. Get yourself relaxed with meditation, breathing, muscle relaxation, or doing something you enjoy that relaxes you, such as reading, gardening, or getting in a hot tub or hot bath.

2. Think about your worry, keeping your mind open to possible solutions. If negative thoughts are interfering, then go to step 3.

3. (Optional) After each thought, label it as "helpful" or "not helpful." Most of the time, when you are thinking thoughts that aren't helpful and you label them as such, those thoughts will decrease and even go away. This clears the mind to make way for more helpful thoughts.

Another way to problem-solve is to brainstorm all possible solutions. The more people we involve in brainstorming solutions, the more likely we are to reach the best solution. Creativity experts have taught us two things about problem-solving: (1) We will come up with a better and more complete list if we work independently first and bring our list together with the lists of others later than if we work together at the start. (2) When we include unethical, illegal, and impractical solutions, it gets the creative juices flowing. This helps us to arrive at better ideas that *are* practical, legal, and ethical than if we begin by restricting our list to only solutions we are prepared to use. When you have a worry or concern that is amenable to problem-solving, use the following worksheet for yourself and as many people as you'd like to involve.

Solving a
Specific Problem

What is a worry that you have that you believe is amenable to problem-solving?

_____

What have you tried so far to solve your problems?

_____

Brainstorm below all possible things you could do, even if they are illegal, unethical, or impractical. Remember that including these ideas can help to fuel greater creativity and lead to more useful ideas.

Optional: Give this worksheet to one or more friends or family members to complete independently of you.

Ideas:

1. _____
2. _____
3. _____
4. _____
5. _____
6. _____
7. _____
8. _____
9. _____
10. _____
11. _____
12. _____
13. _____
14. _____
15. _____

Now cross off all the ideas on all the lists that you do not want to do, including those that are unethical or illegal. From those remaining, circle the ones you like the most.

Can you combine or tweak them? Or perhaps you would like to create a stepwise solution starting with the easiest. For example, maybe you'll start with number 3 and if that doesn't work you'll try number 6.

The previous worksheet is best for a specific problem that you are worried about. The worksheet on the next page is better for recurrent or everyday worries—that is, things like work, children, or what others think of you. These are things you may worry about on a regular or semiregular basis.

The next worksheet, How to Prevent Worry From Interfering is particularly useful when you are about to engage in an activity and you are concerned that worry will interfere with that activity. Some examples of times that worry can interfere with your life include when you are lying down to sleep, studying, enjoying an evening with friends, reading for pleasure, watching a movie or TV show, and completing any task that involves concentration.

Regardless of the activity, there are three choices that you can make before engaging in it: do something about the worry before the activity, plan to do something after it, or do nothing.

I encourage you to do the worksheet when you're concerned worry may interfere with something you are about to do. Once you get good at it, you can try to skip the worksheet and go straight to integrating the things you are planning to do into your to-do list or calendar.

Note: If you complete this next worksheet for insomnia, it is best that you do it at least one hour before bed but not so early in the day that new worries are likely to arise.

SAMPLE WORKSHEET

How to Prevent Worry from Interfering

Here is an example of a completed worksheet for someone who is concerned that their worry will interfere with their sleep:

What I'm likely to worry about in bed	What I want to do about it before bed
My to-do list	Make tomorrow's to-do list and put in planned order
In-laws' visit next month	Call Annie (cleaning person) for 8th, 9th, or 10th Tomorrow: ask to take day off work on Friday 10th to grocery shop, etc.
Afraid I'll be laid off	Nothing

How to Prevent Worry
from Interfering

Do this any time you think worry will interfere with something (e.g., sleep, studying, enjoying friends). In the first column, write what you think you may worry about during that time. In the second column, write what you want to do about it before that event. You have three choices:

1. **Do Something:** do something specific about it before the event.

2. **Plan Something:** plan to do something after the event or another day (record it in your calendar).

3. **Do Nothing:** decide that you've given it "due diligence" and you don't want to do anything at all about it. If you complete this worksheet for insomnia, it is best that you do it at least one hour before bed, but not so early in the day that new worries are likely to arise.

What I'm likely to worry about	What I want to do about it before

6 | Postpone Worry
Chapter

The white bear research (see Chapter 2) taught us that we are terrible at not worrying. **Not only do our attempts to *not* worry fail but they can also cause us to think about our troubles even more, thereby increasing anxiety and depression.** However, we are actually pretty good at postponing worry. There are two general ways in which postponing can be effective. One is for a recurring worry such as work or children. The other is for the occasional big event that someone may worry about for days, weeks, or even months in advance. In the previous chapter, you learned to plan something specific as a way to problem-solve. Postponing is similar, but instead of planning a specific thing to do (e.g., "I'll call my son's teacher tomorrow on my lunch break") you make a decision to think about your concern later (e.g., "I'm going to worry about work on my commute Monday morning").

Regardless of whether you intend to use postponing on a regular basis or as an intermittent strategy, the steps are similar:

1. Make a decision that you do not want to think about this now.

2. Decide when you want to address your concern. Aim for problem-solving rather than worry.

3. Engage in a coping strategy to help let go of the worry.

4. When the worry comes up anyway, gently remind yourself that you are postponing the worry to the time you set aside and repeat the coping strategy.

5. Follow through with addressing the concern when that time comes around. Otherwise, the strategy may not be effective in the future. At this time, aim for solutions or a decision, instead of worrying.

So, let's say that you are eating dinner with your family and you start to worry about work. You decide that you are going to think about this the next morning, on your 20-minute commute to work. You gently shift your attention to focusing on the smell of the food and the temperature and taste of what you are eating and drinking. When you get in the car the next morning, you address the concern and aim toward planning and problem-solving instead of worrying. For these types of worries use the upcoming Postponing Recurrent Worries worksheet.

Let's say that your in-laws are planning a visit for the four-day Thanksgiving weekend. It's August and you're already worrying about it. Pick up the calendar and think about when you want to begin planning for Thanksgiving. After looking at the calendar, you decide that you are likely going to begin planning the Saturday before Thanksgiving, which is November 16. Anytime you begin worrying before that, gently remind yourself that you are going to think about that on November 16. Follow this with a coping strategy as needed. For this type of worry, use the Postponing Worry About an Event on page 26.

The goal is not to completely eradicate worry; rather, it's to find a way to manage your worry so that it doesn't significantly interfere with your functioning and enjoyment of life. **The goal is to significantly reduce the frequency, intensity, and length of time spent worrying.** Nonetheless, with postponing, you have more control over when you are going to address these thoughts rather than them controlling you. In short, the goal is to pare worry down to a normal amount.

Tips:

- If this is working well for recurring worries, try decreasing the frequency or length of your worry or problem-solving periods, or maybe both.

- If it isn't working well for recurring worries, make sure you give each session sufficient time to either get bored or find a resolution. Alternatively, try increasing the frequency or length of your sessions.

- Don't expect perfection. We think over 2,000 thoughts per hour on average. Also, the average healthy person worries 5–10% of the time. Therefore, it is best to accept the worries when they arise, with the goal of significantly reducing their frequency, intensity, and length.

For worries that involve a specific event or change in the future, a slightly different approach is needed. In an example based loosely on a real person, Pierre (a pseudonym) couldn't decide whether to return to his home country. He entered therapy early in March because he was very worried about making the right decision. He was so distressed with this worry that it was interfering with his concentration at work, his sleep, and kept causing him to feel very irritable. Thinking through all the pros and cons left him just as confused and he was unable to stop contemplating the issue. When I asked him when was the soonest he could possibly move back if he knew he was going to return home, he said November. Then I asked him when he'd start preparing for the move. He said the earliest he could apply for a visa would be October 1 and that it would take about a month for the visa to be approved. He agreed to wait until September 15 to start contemplating the decision and wrote a note in his calendar.

Anytime he started to worry about his decision, he said to himself, "I will begin worrying about this on September 15." This proved to be helpful in decreasing his worry and symptoms. I never found out whether Pierre returned home, because his anxiety and depression lifted by early summer. Postponing had been a helpful strategy for him. Other examples of worries for which you can use the postponing technique are starting school, giving a speech, visiting relatives, choosing a college, or deciding on when to retire or whether to move.

Another option for dealing with a worry is to repeatedly postpone it for a week, a month, a quarter, or any other chunk of time until a decision is made. If we have a big decision to make but no fixed date for it, such as whether to retire, whether to buy a car, or another decision that you are indecisive about, you can limit the amount of time you think about it by deciding *not* to decide for a specific time period. For example, if Pierre had been free to move anytime, he could have postponed his decision to the first Saturday of the month, the start of the next quarter, or another time period. Sometimes there is no clear, correct answer and contemplating for hours isn't going to get you any closer to a decision.

When you postpone your worries, you are controlling them, and often life brings you answers in between worry sessions as life changes or more information arises. When the date comes to which you postponed your worry, take time to contemplate, do research, or write about the decision. Continue to postpone until a decision is made. Write the date that you are going to contemplate in your calendar.

Postponing
Recurring Worries

1. What is your recurring worry (or worries) that you find difficult to control?

   _____

   _____

2. In the past week, approximately how much time do you think you worried about this on average per day?

   _____

3. Thinking about due diligence to problem-solve or process your emotions, how much time do you *want* to devote to thinking about this concern in a day? (I recommend that this number be between 5% and 10% of the current estimate, and at least 10 minutes.)

   _____

   _____

4. When do you want to think about this? Good times include on your commute (or a portion of your commute if it is long), during your kids' nap time, during your shower, on a walk, or when you would normally worry most about this anyway.

   _____

   _____

5. Write it in your schedule. Give the worry your full verbal attention. When we worry and when we problem-solve, we typically use the opposite side of our brain (the verbal side—usually the left side) from when we drive (the visual–spatial side—usually the right side). Therefore, most people feel safe addressing concerns while driving, and people who worry excessively usually worry while driving anyway. However, if this doesn't feel safe, choose another time.

6. When the worry arises outside of your designated time:
   a. Note the worry; taste it (remember not to fight it).
   b. Remind yourself of when you will address it.
   c. Gently apply a strategy for letting go of the worry. What is the strategy or strategies you will use to help manage the thoughts?

   _____

   _____

7. After a week…how is this working?

   _____

   _____

Postponing Worry
About an Event

1. What is the event that you are worrying about?

   _____

   _____

   _____

2. What do you want to do to prepare for this event beforehand?

   _____

   _____

   _____

   _____

3. When will you start preparing for the event?

   _____

   - If there is more than one step to preparing for this event, write each one in your calendar now.

   - Anytime you start to worry about the event, remind yourself that you are postponing your worry to the selected date. Follow this with a brief coping strategy.

   - (Optional) If your worry is about making a decision, write down a date to start contemplating, gathering information, researching, and so on. You may choose to set aside regular times to address it by using the previous worksheet.

7 | Being in the Now:
Chapter | Mindfulness

I'd like for you to take a moment to consider when you feel most relaxed. Is it when you're watching a movie? On a hike? Gardening? Cooking? Reading?

Most likely you are realizing that, when you are most relaxed, you are in the present. All worry is about the future. Even when it's about the past, it's often about how it's affecting your future. Often people who are depressed spend a significant amount of time focused on past regrets. Thinking about how things might have been different, and particularly experiencing guilt, can contribute to down moods. Unless there is something that you want to do to rectify the past regrets, it's useless, and there is a clear advantage to being in the moment.

When we fully focus on the moment, we are in the present. Most of the time, the present is free of worry and troubles. Focusing on your senses is the way to free yourself from anxiety about the future and depression about the past and future.

When anything is truly awful in the present, we are typically not worrying. Rather, we are responding to the situation—often in a healthy way that fits the circumstances. Sometimes in these situations, anxiety can be helpful to motivate us to protect ourselves.

Some people believe that worry can motivate them to achieve more. Likewise, these individuals often worry that if they get too relaxed they will lose their edge. However, think about work for a moment. Think about when you are getting things done around the house. Remember that great feeling of being "on a roll," focused, at peak performance. Again, put the book down for a moment and recall what it feels like to be at peak performance. During these times, are you mostly in the past, in the present, or in the future?

Productivity does involve some planning and consideration of the future. Certainly, a little bit of reflection can be useful to enable us to learn from past mistakes. However, we are most productive when we are in the moment. Whether at work, crossing things off our to-do list at home, or engaged in another project, peak performance with all tasks is achieved when we are primarily in the present. Not convinced? Next time you are feeling at peak performance, notice how much of the time you are in the present vs. how much time your mind is on the past or the future.

Mindfulness of Senses

Make a list of at least three to five things that you like to do that you find relaxing:

1. _____

2. _____

3. _____

4. _____

5. _____

Think about when you are engaged in each activity. Take a few seconds to close your eyes and visualize yourself engaged in this activity; put the book down for this exercise.

While doing these things, do you think you are mostly (check one):

In the past? _____

In the present? _____

In the future? _____

List your two favorites below. Check the senses you notice while engaging in each:

1. _____

    ☐ Sight _____

    ☐ Sound _____

    ☐ Physical Sensation _____

    ☐ Smell _____

    ☐ Taste _____

2. _____

    ☐ Sight _____

    ☐ Sound _____

    ☐ Physical Sensation _____

    ☐ Smell _____

    ☐ Taste _____

Now, in the space to the right of the senses you checked above, write one to three things you usually experience with each sense. Have you been mindful of all your senses when doing these things? Closing your eyes, take another moment to imagine yourself in the situation, being mindful of all your available senses. If you discovered additional sensations you weren't noticing before, add them to the list. Next time you're engaged in these activities, remember to notice all your senses.

EXERCISE General Mindfulness

Feeling the book in your hands. Noticing where you are touching the book. Noticing the black words on the light page. Noticing what you see in your periphery. In a moment, when you are ready, put the book down, noticing colors, shapes, and textures.

In a moment, adding awareness of patterns, shadows and highlights. Do this now.

Noticing the sounds that you hear indoors and outdoors, as you are reading this. Can you hear the sound of your breathing? If there are many sounds, thinking of these sounds like a symphony with each sound being a different instrument. Whether few or many sounds, closing your eyes to take a moment to listen.

In a moment, closing your eyes and seeing the backs of your eyelids, while also noticing the sounds that you hear.

Noticing where your hands are touching your book. As you continue reading, noticing the surfaces beneath you, the floor, chair, couch. Also, noticing any surface behind you. Becoming aware of the position of your arms and legs and where they are touching one another. Noticing the feeling of your socks, shoes, clothing, and jewelry.

You can use the free recording "General Mindfulness." This recording may be used at any time, but it probably works best when you are sitting quietly. Find at least five minutes each day to engage in a mindful activity. It may be something that you are already doing, or it might be time you carve out of each day. If you already walk, run, garden, or cook, you can use these activities and similar activities for your mindfulness activity.

Alternatively, or in addition, plan at least a five-minute walk or take five minutes to sit outside or to look out of a window. It is better if you can set aside more time, but if I ask you to do 30 minutes you may not do it at all. When indoors, you can add aromatherapy, instrumental music, or a nature recording. Consider watching a nature DVD on mute, with or without music that you add.

Once your mindfulness skill has developed, you can use it to remain in the moment for most of your day. Become more mindful of beauty on a daily basis. While walking to and from your car, sitting at a stoplight, walking to public transportation, or on the bus or train, become more aware of nature. Noticing the sky and clouds, the sound of the wind and the birds, the feeling of the sun and the breeze. Also becoming more aware of the beauty in architecture and in other human-made things that are pleasing to the eye, such as fabric and art.

You can use the free recordings or scripts to help guide you and train you to be in the moment, thereby becoming mindful. The next free recording is "Walking Mindfulness." The recording is more involved and longer than the script. However, all the ideas in the recording are included in the walking exercises that follow the script.

EXERCISE   Walking Mindfulness

To prepare for these walks, wear shoes suitable for walking and go outside. If you are a runner, you can use the recording while running too. Plan a time that you'd like to take a mindfulness walk using the free "Walking Mindfulness" track, or using the information in the script below. If using the recording, leave one earbud out so you can hear what is around you.

Script: *Beginning by focusing on what you see. Noticing the colors, shapes, and textures of plants, buildings, cars [pause]. Noticing the trees, seeing the colors and movement of the trees from the wind [pause]. Noticing the colors and any movement in the sky: clouds, birds, planes. As you begin to focus on the horizon, watching how the landscape is changing as you move forward [pause]. Feeling your movements, your muscles contracting in your legs, the swinging in your arms. Noticing how the earth below you feels as your feet touch the ground. Feeling the rhythm of your movements [pause]. Noticing the feeling of the breeze. Focusing all your attention on the breeze, noticing how it feels. Noticing how it moves trees, plants, your hair, the clouds [pause]. Noticing the sound of the breeze in your ear and noticing whether you can hear it moving leaves, wind chimes, or something else [pause]. Noticing other things that you might hear, such as the sounds of birds, cars, crickets, dogs [pause]. Noticing if there is something that you smell [pause]. Allowing your mind to float gently between your senses.*

Walk 1

What did you discover from going on this mindful walk?

What thoughts distracted you from staying in the moment?

What strategies from previous chapters did you use to deal with those thoughts that distracted you?

What strategies from previous chapters would you like to use to deal with unwanted thoughts in the future?

On your next mindful walks, take some of the time to experiment with the following.

Walk 2: Take a Non-Judgmental Stance
While it may be impossible to do this fully, your goal is to avoid thinking of anything as positive or negative while observing your senses. For instance, fumes are not nasty, people are not ugly, homes are not pretty. This non-judgmental stance includes times that you begin to worry or otherwise stray from the moment; it's not bad, it just is. When thoughts interfere, remember that perfection is not the goal and accepting imperfection is.

Walk 3: Like a Baby
A baby can experience all their senses but has no words for their experiences. Observing only the raw sensations without labels on your next walk. Expect that you will have some labels but, to the extent possible, observing your senses like a baby would.

Walk 4: One Sense, Two Senses, or All Senses?
Observe how you feel while you are focusing on each sense. Which sense is your favorite? Your second favorite?

Also on walk 4, experiment focusing on one sense at a time, allowing the others to fall into the background even though you'll be aware of them. Next focusing on two senses at a time. Then allowing your mind to float freely between your senses. If you prefer one or two at a time, you can still vary them. For instance, you may begin by focusing on sight and sound, then move to focusing on sound and physical sensation, then to physical sensation and smell. In fact, your experiences may guide you. For example, you might be noticing the sounds of birds singing and feeling the ground beneath you when you feel, see, and hear the breeze increasing, so you switch to physical sensation and sound. When the breeze settles, perhaps you smell someone barbecuing. The wonderful aromas motivate you to switch to smell while still feeling the gentler breeze.

After walk 4, were you able to focus on the moment *most* of the time?

If you believe you were in the moment at least 75% of the time or if you are content with how it went (e.g., you thought about pleasant things from the past or future, and/or you worried significantly less than usual), you can skip the advice for walk 5.

Walk 5: Labeling Your Experiences
On your next walk, when you notice that you are unable to disengage from worries, label your experiences. For example, "*birds singing, sound of feet, colorful flowers, smell of flowers, hearing wind in the trees, feeling the wind, blue sky, white clouds, car exhaust, lamp post, dog barking, green grass.*" Once you feel you are in the present, go back to focusing on your senses like a baby would. When thoughts interfere, briefly taste the worry and gently shift back to the present, using thought labeling as needed.

Over the course of the next few days, engage in most of the activities listed on the next form and describe what your experience was like. While participating in each of these activities, your goal is to be focusing on your senses. However, we are thinkers. Therefore, expect that thoughts will interfere and, when they do, acknowledge the thought (rather than trying to push it out of the way) and "gently shifting your attention back to the moment."

Self-Monitoring of Mindful Activities

In the first column there are a number of activities in which you can mindfully engage. In the second column, write a description of your experiences while you engaged in the activity (e.g., I never realized how great my shampoo smells. I really enjoyed feeling and listening to the water too. I loved how relaxed I felt during and after the shower.) In the third column, write the percentage of time you felt like you were in the moment.

Activity	Description of Mindful Activity	% of Time in the Moment
Example: Shower, in particular paying attention to the smells of your soap, shampoo, etc.		
Take at least a 10-minute walk, focusing particularly on nature		
Take at least a 10-minute drive. Unsafe? No! You are safest while being mindful of what you see and hear		
Do the dishes, paying particular attention to the suds		
If you are sexually active, engage in sexual activity focusing on your senses rather than anticipating climax		
Weather permitting, sit outside; alternatively, sit on a bench in a mall, or sit in a coffee shop by a window		
Create a mindfully-rich experience: get a piece of chocolate and a favorite beverage, and play instrumental music; light a candle or incense and watch it; or look outside or at a piece of art		

While it would be nice to record a 90% or 100% in the 3rd column, any improvement over what you currently do while engaged in these activities is progress. For instance, if while you are showering, you typically worry 80% of the time and are only in the moment 20% of the time, being in the moment even 40% of the time is a big improvement. Celebrate even small accomplishments!

Many people listen to music while on a walk, while showering, while eating, and so on. It's good for the soul to sing! However, when engaging in mindfulness, it's generally preferred to listen to the sounds around you. Alternatively, choose instrumental music, without words (chant is fine).

EXERCISE Start Making Scents

Smell reaches the amygdala, the emotional center of the brain, directly. The other four senses are first processed in the frontal lobes of the brain, which are responsible for higher mental processes. Therefore, smells are much more likely to trigger an emotional response than any of the other senses.

This emotional response makes the senses much more likely to be conditioned to events. For instance, if a woman is raped by a cigar smoker, the smell of cigars is very likely to elicit fear and trigger a flashback.

The same is true of pleasant scents. That is, smell can have a more immediate and profound relaxing effect than other senses. We can even learn to enjoy smells that most others find unpleasant due to conditioning. That is, if an otherwise unpleasant smell occurs at the same time as a very emotionally positive event, we can learn to love that smell. Perhaps the most common example of this is when people enjoy the smell of manure because it's associated with happy times at a family member's farm.

1. Choose a scent that you find pleasant. Find at least one of the following (preferably two or three) that has a similar or the same scent: a lotion, an essential oil, an incense, a spray, or a candle. You can purchase essential oils in some health-food stores (such as Whole Foods), Dollar Tree, some vitamin stores, some boutiques, and online.

2. If using an essential oil or spray, find an old dishrag, towel, or worn-out piece of clothing. Cut or tear a very small piece of the cloth (about one and a half or two inches square) and put a few drops of oil on it or saturate it with spray. To protect other things from the oil, wrap a larger piece of dry cloth around the scented cloth and secure it with a rubber band. The aroma will penetrate through the cloth but the oil won't. If you can't smell it, you either put too little essential oil on the scented cloth or you put too much dry cloth around it. You can also burn an essential oil or put it in diffusers around your house and in your office.

3. When you are relaxed, smell the cloth or use the lotion, spray, candle, or incense. The goal is to condition yourself to associate the smell with relaxation. One way is to pair your scent with times when you are relaxed organically (e.g., reading or watching TV). Another way is to practice quiet relaxation at home, put your chosen aromatherapy at arm's length when you begin, and then once you feel relaxed add the smell. Do this at least three times before going on to the next step.

4. Once you're conditioned to the smell, keep your aromatherapy with you and smell it when you're feeling stressed.

5. Continue to pair it with relaxation so that it remains a cue for relaxation, rather than one of stress.

8 | Better-But-Believable Thinking

Chapter 8

Cognitive therapy was initially developed to treat depression, but it helps substantially with anxiety and other troublesome emotions too. Sometimes emotions are normal, healthy reactions to life's circumstances (see Chapter 11, on acceptance of healthy emotion). When we feel unhealthy levels of anxiety, depression, guilt, frustration, or embarrassment, it's usually because we are thinking negatively. **In fact, we can argue that there are truly no unhealthy emotions, only unhealthy thoughts leading to unnecessary painful emotions.**

Cognitive therapy is a way to systematically change negative thoughts into more healthy thoughts to manage unhealthy emotions. You may have tried positive thinking, and sometimes that can be helpful. However, if it worked very well, you probably wouldn't be reading this right now. The problem with positive thinking is that if you don't believe the positive thoughts are true, they won't be helpful. In fact, some people complain that trying to think positively is an exercise in frustration that can even lead to feeling hopeless. **This is the first problem with cognitive therapy: positive thinking doesn't help if it isn't believable.**

Traditional cognitive therapists begin by asking you to identify negative thoughts that generate depression and anxiety. Next, they expect you to learn several faulty thinking styles and identify what type of error in thinking you are engaging in that is causing that emotion (e.g., catastrophizing, emotional reasoning, or filtering). The next step is to read what you are supposed to do to change this thought in a positive direction by looking at an index with specific instructions for how to combat each thought style. The final step is to construct a new, better thought that will reduce or eliminate your anxiety or depression about the original negative thought. **This is the second problem with cognitive therapy: the number and complexity of the steps involved to reach the better thought means the process is often abandoned due to the time and energy involved to arrive at the new thought.**

The solution to both problems with cognitive therapy is "better-but-believable thoughts," or "B³s." They are called "B³s" because each of the three words starts with the letter "B," and it's catchy! Instead of going through all the preceding steps or reaching for the most positive thought that isn't believable, think of an alternative thought that is *better* than the depressing or anxiety-producing thought, yet believable. For instance, if a teen baseball player is feeling depressed because he struck out twice and made an error, he could think, "Even my favorite major league players have struck out twice and made an error in some games" or "The last game, I hit a double and a homer and made no errors, so I know I can do that again." Or, if a father is worried about his young son driving, he might think, "Millions of 16-year-olds drive safely every day" or "There's a greater than 99% chance he'll come home safely tonight" or "Worrying won't bring him home safely—I'll postpone my worry to if there is an accident." B³s are meant to be simple. Therefore, most of the time a worksheet isn't necessary. You can just think of B³s on the fly. When you are feeling anxious, depressed, or frustrated, note whether you are thinking negatively and, if so, come up with at least one B³. The more B³s you can create, the greater the likelihood that you'll feel better.

Again, this is a simple technique. However, when a thought is particularly depressing or anxiety-producing or you have a particularly difficult time with a re-occurring negative thought, the following worksheet can be helpful. To improve its effectiveness, have your therapist, a friend, or a family member complete the sheet as well. Because we make better and more complete lists if we work separately, avoid sharing your worksheets until you've come up with as many B³s as you can think of individually.

Better-But-Believable
Thoughts (B³s)

Step One

What are the negative thought(s) that are causing you to feel anxious, depressed, or otherwise distressed?

_____

_____

Step Two

What is the opposite of that thought? Or, what is the most positive thing you can think instead of the negative thought?

_____

_____

Step Three

Brainstorm several other thoughts that are better than your negative thought but more believable than the thought you wrote down under step two. Think of at least five B³s about your situation or concern that are better than your negative thoughts but that you believe are true. Be creative! Think outside the box on creative B³s rather than staying focused on the opposite.

1. _____

2. _____

3. _____

4. _____

5. _____

6. _____

7. _____

8. _____

9. _____

10. _____

Step Four

Now read aloud each B^3 from all the lists, paying careful attention to how you feel when you say it. Also consider how helpful you believe it will be as time progresses. Cross off the sentences that aren't helpful.

Step Five

Go back and read each one again, rating it on a scale of 2–10, with 2 being only a little helpful and 10 being very helpful.

Step Six

Cross off all the B^{3}s that have ratings at the lower end of the scale, leaving you with the B^{3}s that are the most helpful.

Step Seven

Choose two to four B^{3}s. In choosing the statements, consider how high their ratings are, but also try to choose ones that will help in a variety of ways. For instance, in the baseball example, if you rated "I've been told I'm a very talented player" as a 7 and "I usually play much better than I did today" as an 8, you might still choose "I really love playing the game" over the first B^{3}s, even if you only rated it as a 6, because it is significantly different from the other two examples.

Moving forward, anytime you feel anxious or depressed, assess whether a B^3 might help you feel better. Sometimes it's not even necessary to identify the negative thought. What's more important than identifying a negative thought is whether thinking a good or neutral but believable thought helps you to feel better.

If you use the "Problem-solving" worksheet in Chapter 5, it may be more useful if you add a B^{3}s column to that worksheet, as seen on the next page. Write these B^{3}s in your devices, on a notecard, or memorize them.

Problem-Solving

The first two columns of this sheet are the same the Problem-Solving Worksheet on p. 22. You may continue to use that worksheet anytime you are concerned about worry interfering with sleep, studying, etc.

Use this sheet instead when you think that adding B^3s about your worries may help.

What I'm likely to worry about _____	What I want to do about it before _____*	Better-but-believable thoughts

* Options for column two are: (1) do something before bed, (2) plan to do something another day (specify when and record it in your calendar), or (3) do nothing.

9 | Stop Should-ing on Yourself

Chapter

Most of us overuse words and phrases such as "I should," "I need to," and "I have to." For some, it causes a great deal of anxiety and depression. Sometimes these words are completely inaccurate—in reality, the person does have the option to *not* do the thing they say they have to do, should do, or need to do. Most of the time, these words at least exaggerate reality. After all, the only things we really need to do are eat, sleep, breathe, and have somewhere sheltered to live.

Perhaps the most important things to remember about the imperatives we tell ourselves, and often tell others, is that there is usually a choice and there is almost always something that we *want* to do that is involved with the task. In a way, this is another B³ (see Chapter 8). By changing a "need to" situation into a "want to" situation, we often relieve anxiety while simultaneously increasing motivation. **First of all, "need to" and "have to" are commands that create tension, and "should" doesn't feel much better.** Furthermore, I believe there's a bit of a child in all of us such that when we are told that we "need to" do something, we don't want to do it, even if it's a self-imposed "need to."

Think about Tom Sawyer whitewashing the fence in Mark Twain's novel. He turned a job into a privilege by getting people to believe that they really *wanted* to do this work. Imagine if he told people they *needed* to whitewash the fence. How many takers do you think he would have enticed?

In addition to finding the "want to" in every situation, we can introduce some flexibility in how the task is accomplished. Let's say that your floors are dirty. You initially think, "I *need* to sweep, mop, and vacuum." If you changed that to "I *want* to sweep, mop, and vacuum," that would be unlikely to be helpful because most people don't like to do housework so it would be a lie. What *do* you want? You want your floors to be clean. If you change your thought to "I *want* my floors to be clean," it's true and more motivating. You could also think, "I want to cross it off my list, because I'll feel better when it's done." Experiment with a variety of "coulds" as well: "I could clean them tomorrow," "I could hire a cleaning person," "I could make it a condition of my kids' allowance," "I could get my spouse to share the tasks," or "I could vacuum today and sweep and mop tomorrow."

On a day-to-day basis, be mindful of how often you say these imperatives. If you aren't certain about this, ask family, close friends, and perhaps colleagues if you overuse these words. If you do overuse these words, think about how they may be affecting your children, spouse, colleagues, and friends—particularly if you are "should-ing" on them. Consider whether you would like for others to gently let you know when you are using imperatives. Think about who you could get feedback from without feeling defensive and how you'd like for them to let you know.

Finding "The Want"

In the left-hand column, make a list of things you haven't done that you are feeling like you *should* do or are telling yourself that you *need* to do or *have* to do. Then, in the right-hand column, write at least one sentence for each of the statements on the left, changing them so that they contain the words "want to" and/or "could."

Should Do, Need to Do, or Have to Do	Want To or Could

Focusing on the place in your body where you feel anxiety or tension, read one of the statements in the column on the left. If you are alone, say it aloud. How does it feel?

_____

_____

Focusing on the same place in your body, read your alternative *want to* and *could* statements. How does it feel? How motivated are you to get started?

_____

_____

Continue down the list, reading each of your original statements and alternative sentences aloud.

Exploring Alternatives
to "Shoulds"

In the event that the previous exercise is ineffective, this more involved worksheet may be more helpful. Below is a sample worksheet for someone who doesn't like to work out but enjoys the benefits of working out. **On the next page there is a blank worksheet for you to use.**

What is the "should/need to" statement?

I need to work out.

What will happen if I don't do it?

I'll be sorry that I skipped it and may not sleep as well tonight.

What is the "want to"?

I want to have that great feeling I do after I leave the gym. I want to be healthy. I want to sleep well. I want to keep my weight down without worrying too much about how much I eat. I want to be strong.

When else could I do it or what are the alternatives?

I could go in-line skating or go for a bike ride. I could even go for a walk. In the future, I could join a tennis league or get a friend to exercise with me.

What would make it more pleasant?

Taking some good tunes and a tasty sports drink. I could find a class that I like more than lifting weights and being on the cardio machines.

Will I be glad that I did it?

I'm always glad that I went!

Reframed "want to" statement(s):

I will be glad that I went to the gym because I feel more relaxed, sleep better, and can enjoy my lunch more. It's good for my mental and physical health. Therefore, I really do want to go to the gym.

Exploring Alternatives
to "Shoulds"

What is the "should/need to" statement?

_____

_____

What will happen if I don't do it?

_____

_____

What is the "want to"?

_____

_____

When else could I do it or what are the alternatives?

_____

_____

What would make it more pleasant?

_____

_____

Will I be glad that I did it?

_____

_____

Reframed "want to" statement(s):

_____

_____

10 | Everything in Moderation:
Chapter | Avoid the Extremes

Remember that you feel what you think. If you say, "Nothing ever goes right for me," you will feel like nothing ever goes right for you. If you say, "I can't do anything right," you will feel like you can't do anything right. Some other common extreme words and phrases that can leave you feeling angry, frustrated, anxious, and sad include "everything," "always," "never," "every time," "constantly," "horrible," and "bad." In the example of "I can't do anything right," it's more accurate to say something like "I'm frustrated that I'm making an unusual number of mistakes today. I know I can do better." The good news is that this bad habit of using extreme words can be changed.

When you use extreme words and change them to something more accurate, you feel better. One example is saying that you "hate" something or someone, when the reality is that you dislike it or dislike them. If you use the word "hate" daily, it's likely you use it when you don't really mean it. However, you will feel like you do hate many of the aspects of your life and this will affect your mood accordingly. If you only use the word "hate" once or twice a week (when you truly mean it), it will have a greater impact when you use it to express yourself to others too. Similarly, when you say it frequently, people may perceive you as a negative person. Moreover, when you use more moderate and accurate labels, the things that you only dislike won't feel quite as bad as when you use the word "hate."

Another example is the word "never." Some examples in sentences are "You never help me," "I never do anything right," "You never support me," and "You never visit me anymore." A very similar misuse is seen in its opposite: the word "always." Some examples are "You always criticize me," "You always come home late," "You always watch TV," and "I always have bad luck."

EXERCISE   Extreme Words

Below on the left are some of the words that are overused that can add to depression, anger, and anxiety. To the right are words and thoughts that you may want to substitute instead of those words. When in doubt, ask yourself which is more accurate: one of the words on the left or one of the words on the right.

Circle those extreme words that you think you may use inaccurately.

Extreme Words	Substitute Words and Thoughts
Hate	Dislike, Don't like
Always	Often
Never	Not often enough, Rarely
Constantly	Frequently, More often than I'd like, Usually
Awful, Terrible, Horrible	Unfortunate, Uncomfortable
Worthless, Loser	Find ways in which you or the other person is worthwhile; be more specific about the shortcoming that caused you to think the extreme word.
Failure	You are *not* a failure! Unsuccessful events are temporary and serve as learning experiences. It's a fact that failures are positively correlated with success: people who try and fail are more likely to succeed in the long term. There's a difference between failing at something and letting it define you as a failure.

Some phrases I often hear that are examples of extreme thoughts are: "I'm having a bad day," "My life sucks" and "She's an idiot" or "I'm an idiot." Another one is "I have the worst luck" when, in reality, there have certainly been times when the speaker had good things happen to them. In some instances, we may recognize that these words aren't accurate but say them anyway to blow off steam. If you think you do this, be sure to be mindful of the reality.

There are exceptions to these rules; otherwise, we would not have these words in the English language. Sometimes extreme words "fit." The first thing to consider is how the use of these words feel when you are saying or thinking them. The second thing to consider is whether the use of these words is accurate or an exaggeration. Is the use of the word extreme or true? If eating blue cheese literally makes you gag, you hate blue cheese. If your child has cancer, it is truly awful. If a terrorist murders 25 innocent people, it's horrible. If you miss an appointment, it's not awful, it's unfortunate. If you get into a fender-bender, it's not horrible, it's frustrating.

If there have been no instances ever of you oversleeping, you can say "I never oversleep." In addition, if you *rarely* oversleep, it's okay to say or think that you *never* oversleep. While it would be more accurate to say "rarely," it's certainly not necessary to change exaggerated words if they don't cause you, or someone who hears them, to feel uncomfortable. In fact, if you're an optimist, it might be that you use extreme words inaccurately but that they make you feel good, and in this case, there is certainly no need to change them unless you are misinforming someone.

If your thought is pessimistic and inaccurate, it will likely contribute to you feeling worse about a situation. For example, if you're running late and hit unexpected traffic and you think, "This is horrible," you're likely to *feel* like it is horrible. Even if you're going to an important interview, it's not horrible. If you substitute the word "unfortunate" for "horrible," you will likely feel much better. If you think of the situation as frustrating and unfortunate, when you arrive, you're likely to explain your lateness better and sound better in terms of your voice tone and facial expressions. Once the interview begins, you're likely to be more composed in your interview than if you're thinking, "Oh no, this is the worst! This is horrible. I'm feeling awful!"

The most important thing to consider is whether there is another word that is true, but feels better or sounds better than saying the more extreme word. Imagine that you're running late to an interview and say aloud "Getting stuck in this traffic is horrible" while thinking about arriving late. Now think about arriving late and saying "Getting stuck in this traffic is unfortunate."

Does it sound better and feel better to say "I don't like blue cheese" than it does to say "I hate blue cheese?"

Discovering and Changing
Your Extreme Words

Below, list the words and phrases you tend to use in a way that exaggerates your situation in a negative way and makes you feel worse. It may be helpful to ask others to point out extreme words that you overuse. Consider asking people close to you whether they hear you say some of these extreme words, too.

To the right of each word, write at least one replacement word or rephrase. If it's helpful, write about how these words make you feel and what thoughts and feelings might be more accurate.

Extreme word or phrase	Accurate replacement word or phrase
Never	Rarely — This feels moe hopeful and less frustrating

11
Chapter

Acceptance of Healthy Emotion

Emotions are healthy. Anxiety and anger, in particular, help us to protect ourselves. It's normal to feel sad when we experience loss. While guilt is usually an unhealthy emotion, sometimes feeling guilty can motivate us to be more respectful and mindful of others.

You might find it surprising to learn that people who experience unhealthy levels of anxiety and depression often have a more difficult time accepting *healthy* emotions. In fact, this may be the primary cause of some people's anxiety and depression. Some people refuse to feel healthy emotions and purposefully avoid and repress their emotions—that is, they hold in emotions instead of expressing them in a healthy way. Others repress emotion involuntarily and have difficulty accessing the emotion; they may be unaware that it's there. Either way, repressing emotions has been proven to be particularly unhealthy. In fact, an interesting study on the cognitive treatment of depression (Castonguay, Goldfried, Wiser, Raue, & Hayes, 1996) found that people who express more emotion during the course of therapy enjoy greater improvements than those who hold their emotions in. Similar studies of treatment for anxiety have found that those who hold their emotions in during a course of cognitive–behavioral therapy don't improve as much as those who express their emotions (Newman et al., 2011).

Marsha Linehan (1993), the original developer of dialectical behavioral therapy, refers to our healthy emotions as "primary emotions" and the unhealthy reactions to them as "secondary emotions." Ideally, mindful acceptance of emotions will help us to accept healthy primary emotions, such that we experience them even though they are uncomfortable while also avoiding unnecessary, unhealthy secondary emotions. The best way to identify primary emotions is to ask yourself: "What would almost everyone feel if this happened to them?"

For example, let's say that your dog was playing in the front yard inside an electric fence and a drunken speeder lost control of his car and killed your dog. What are the two emotions that anyone would feel?

1. _____ 2. _____

If you are like most people, you wrote "sadness" or an equivalent such as "grief" or "heartbroken" or "depressed" (I like to think of grief and sadness as healthy emotions and depression as being unhealthy). You also probably wrote "angry," "mad," or a similar emotion such as "livid" or "pissed." If you experienced this situation and you accepted those emotions, it is likely that you would only feel these two emotions. Furthermore, you would be able to process the grief for your dog more quickly, thereby healing more quickly.

If instead you didn't accept your sadness and anger, you would have additional emotions in response to them. For instance, you might get frustrated that you are sad or maybe you would be embarrassed that you cried. You might even get sad that you feel sad, such that your sadness turns into depression. Likewise, you might feel anxious about your anger, or you might feel guilty or embarrassed about expressing it. You might hold your anger in and feel depressed. Then you might feel depressed and hopeless about your guilt and frustrated with your depression.

The secondary emotions can become more intense than the primary emotions, and, moreover, instead of processing the event, you're focused on all the emotions you're feeling and may even forget about why you started feeling all of those emotions in the first place.

Quite often there is a negative thought or judgment about the primary emotion that leads to a secondary emotion. Judgments can include phrases such as "This is awful" and "I can't stand it," but they most often include a "should." You might think that you *shouldn't* feel your emotion or that you should be stronger. However, the reality is that if the emotion you're experiencing is one that most people feel, it is healthiest to allow the feelings even if they are uncomfortable, because the alternative will be much more painful in the long run.

If you believe you have a difficult time accepting your primary emotions, it is recommended that you see a therapist. However, the following worksheet will likely be helpful.

This next worksheet is also helpful for learning to process and express emotions about recent events and events that may occur in the future. Many people who are suffering from anxiety and depression have repressed emotions from past traumatic events. In fact, you may have repressed emotions from difficult times in your life that you wouldn't consider to be traumatic.

In my practice and in conversations with colleagues, I have seen and heard about several clients who finally turned a corner after eventually crying or getting angry about something that happened to them in the past, often decades ago. Speak to your therapist if you think this applies to you. If you do not have a therapist, hopefully you will find this workbook helpful. If you complete the workbook and are not satisfied with your results, it may be that you could really benefit from doing some deeper work to process your emotions with a therapist.

Dealing with
Difficult Emotions

1. List the emotions that you have been struggling with in recent days:

   _____

   _____

2. Now list the event or events that triggered these emotions:

   _____

   _____

3. Circle the emotion or emotions under question 1 that you believe anyone would feel in response to the event or events in question 2. It's okay to get some help from your therapist or a friend for input if you're not certain.

4. What are the "shoulds" or other negative thoughts you have about your primary emotions (the emotions you circled)?

   _____

   _____

   _____

   _____

5. What are some B^{3}s about the emotion or emotions (see Chapter 8)? Include, "It is normal and healthy to feel these emotions."

   _____

   _____

   _____

   _____

6. Close your eyes and get in touch with the memory of the situation (if there is more than one, choose one). Remember the events in as much detail as you can. Allow yourself to feel the emotion or emotions you felt at the time. (If this is overwhelming, wait to do this with the support of a therapist. If you don't have a therapist, please consider finding one.) If it's not overwhelming, do this now.

7. Write what you remember about the event, focusing on your initial emotions. If you felt secondary emotions during the event, be sure to focus on the primary emotions.

_____

_____

_____

_____

8. Talk about the event and your feelings with your therapist, if you have one. Otherwise speak with a trusted friend, family member, or religious leader.

Daily Self-Monitoring 2

Hopefully you are still using the "Daily Self-Monitoring" worksheet from Chapter 1 to keep you on track. This new monitoring form is identical except that it adds another column, "Healthy Emotion." In this additional column, simply list the healthy emotions you experienced during the day. These could be anxiety, irritability, or other healthy emotions (e.g., anger, embarrassment, regret) you experienced in response to difficult circumstances (being treated unfairly, making a mistake). Also use this column to write more positive emotions, such as "happy," "relieved," "connected," and "appreciated."

As in the worksheet in Chapter 1, in the other columns, rate each emotion on a 0–10 scale with a 10 being the most anxious, depressed, or irritable you have ever been and 0 being completely relaxed, very happy, and not at all irritated. If one or two of the emotions aren't problematic, feel free to skip rating them. For "Applying Strategies," you can give yourself a grade (e.g., B+), or rate yourself on a 0–10.

Date	Anxiety	Depression	Irritability	Applying Strategies?	Healthy Emotion
11/1	3	4	NA	B	Sad, Connected, Loved

12 Chapter | Relaxation

Relaxation is an important part of coping with anxiety. Being relaxed is the antithesis of being anxious. This certainly isn't surprising, but do you know that it's also important in dealing with depression? Interestingly, when we used only relaxation techniques with people who suffered from generalized anxiety disorder and felt depressed, their mood improved significantly despite the fact we weren't directly addressing their depression (Borkovec, Abel, & Newman, 1995; Borkovec, Newman, Pincus, & Lytle, 2002).

When using the following relaxation techniques, please remember the blue monkeys (see Chapter 2). In other words, gently move toward relaxation rather than pushing away from anxiety. There are several relaxation scripts to follow. You have three choices. First, you can read the scripts, practice them, and eventually remember what to do. Second, you can read the scripts yourself or have someone read the scripts and record them (see Therapist Chapter 12 for ways to make recordings). Third, you can purchase the recordings of these exercises by going to this webpage: AnxietyStLouisPsychologist.com/free.

Perhaps the most common relaxation technique is breathing. You may have learned to breathe deeply from your diaphragm, or to breathe in through your nose and out through your mouth, or you may have learned to count to a certain number as you breathe in and out. If these work for you, that's great! These techniques are not wrong. However, even if these techniques work well for you, substituting command words with process words (e.g., "breathing" vs. "breathe"), or states, may make the techniques even more effective. Even when using process words with breathing techniques, many people get performance anxiety about whether they are doing it right, thereby increasing their anxiety or impeding relaxation. Still others may find the techniques of limited effectiveness due to the effort involved. With mindful breathing, there is no performance and it's basically effortless, so there is no anxiety.

Breathe In Through Your Nose

Breathe Out Through Your Mouth

EXERCISE Mindful Breathing Plus

1. Read the following and apply it as you are reading:

   Making no effort to breathe in any certain way, instead just observing your breathing [pause]. Following your breathing [pause]. As you begin focusing on your nose, noticing that as you breathe in, the air feels cool, and as you breathe out, the air feels warmer [pause]. Feeling the cool air expanding your lungs as you inhale and noticing the warmer air escaping through your nose as your lungs relax. Noticing if you can hear the sound of the air coming in and out of your nose [pause]. Noticing that just after you breathe out, your body is still before you breathe in. Enjoying that quiet pause. Noticing how still and relaxed your body is between breaths.

2. Closing your eyes, doing the same as above, but instead of thinking of the words, focusing on the raw sensations of your breathing. That is, focusing on the sound, feeling, and physical sensations of your breathing, without labels, like a baby would.

3. Go back to the words you found most relaxing in Chapter 4. Integrate the word or words you found most relaxing into your breathing. For instance, if your best word was "releasing," think this word with your breathing: thinking "re" as you breathe in, "lease" as you breathe out, and "ing" during the quite pause. Or, if you chose "peace" and "soft," you can think "peace" as you inhale, "soft" as you exhale, and just enjoy the quiet pause. Alternatively, you could think "still" or another favorite word during the quiet pause. Create your own two- and three-word phrases to coincide with the three phases of breathing (e.g., "God-is-peace," "Sha-lom," "Love-to-all").

4. Instead of thinking words, visualize colors. As you breathe in, you can choose a relaxing color. Preferably pick a cool color such as blue or aqua, but any color you like is fine. Alternatively, visualize yourself breathing in fresh, clear, oxygenated air. As you breathe out, breathing out a warm color such as yellow or red. Or think about what color your anxiety feels like and breathing out that color. Avoid forcing it out—instead, just allowing the air to escape little by little.

5. During the next quiet pause, thinking the number "5." Thinking "4" during the next quiet pause, and thinking one lower number for each quiet pause between breaths, counting all the way down to zero. When you get to zero, taking one more breath and then opening your eyes. Alternatively, switch to another relaxation strategy.

Experiment by trying various combinations of the above strategies and comparing them with simply observing your breathing.

The Ocean

Most people love the ocean and most associate it with being on vacation. If you prefer the mountains, you can do something similar to this.

1. What is your favorite scenario at the beach? Circle one:

   Early in the morning with the sun rising over the ocean.

   Midday with the sun bright and warm, but with a cooling breeze.

   Sunset with the sunlight reflecting off the water.

   Nighttime with the moon shining brightly, dancing off the waters.

2. In the following spaces, write as many specific sensations you can remember experiencing at the ocean, or mountains, for each sense.

   Sight:

   _____

   Sound:

   _____

   Physical sensation:

   _____

   Smell:

   _____

   Taste:

   _____

3. Find a quiet place. It must be quiet enough for you to hear the sound of your breathing. Soon you can close your eyes. When you do close your eyes after observing your breathing, you will notice that the sound of your breathing sounds very much like waves on the ocean. The following is a sample script, but you can create your own, using your sensations from the time of day you chose. **You may also listen to the optional recording "Ocean."**

   Gently closing your eyes. Begin by focusing on your breathing. Noticing that the sound of your breathing sounds very much like waves on the ocean. As you breathe in, it sounds as if the waves are rolling in and as you breathe out, it's like the ebb is falling back into the ocean [pause]. After the waves fall back into the ocean, there's a quiet pause before the next wave comes in [pause]. Noticing how relaxing it is to be at one with the ocean. Enjoying that your breathing and the ocean feel as one [pause]. Beginning to visualize the waves, if you haven't already. As the waves are rolling in, smelling the fresh salt air, sunscreen, and any other smells you might associate with the beach [pause]. Hearing seagulls and watching them [pause]. Imagining feeling the breeze and a light mist from the ocean as the waves roll toward you. Feeling the warm sun overhead while enjoying a gentle breeze [pause]. Imagining the taste and temperature of a cool drink.

Progressive relaxation is likely the most effective relaxation technique (Bernstein & Borkovec, 1973). It involves systematically tensing and releasing 16 muscle groups. You learn to feel the difference between tension and relaxation and are able to lower your adaptation level (e.g., the amount of tension you use to get through the day). This leads to significantly improved physical and mental health, including a positive effect on sleep, tension headaches, blood pressure, pain, anxiety, sexual satisfaction, premenstrual syndrome, and irritability. It is complex and research has shown that learning it from a trained therapist is much more effective than learning it in a group or on your own from a book.

The next four exercises will be useful in reducing your muscle tension. However, for the best results, it is recommended that you learn progressive relaxation from a therapist who is well-trained in the procedure.

EXERCISE   Sponge (Optional Recording)

It is best if you begin seated with both feet on the floor or lying down.

Closing your eyes and noticing where your body is touching the surfaces beneath you. Feeling the floor beneath your feet, the couch beneath your legs and seat, and the surface or surfaces behind you. Visualizing, imagining, that the surfaces beneath and behind you are like sponges that, instead of absorbing water, absorb tension from your body [pause]. Making no effort to relax. Instead just feeling the absorbing power of the spongy surfaces beneath you [pause]. Allowing gravity to help drain the tension from your body [pause]. Allowing your breathing to help. Each time you breathe in, the tension is loosening, and each time you breathe out, you're feeling a little more relaxed as the tension drains into the spongy surfaces beneath you.

EXERCISE   Tin Man To Scarecrow

This exercise involves tensing all the major muscle groups in the body, like a tin man, and then releasing them, feeling like a scarecrow. Do tense your muscles hard, but, instead of thinking of making them as hard as steel (like Superman), aim for tin to avoid straining your muscles. This should never cause pain.

The following is a list of all the muscle groups. Try these individually as you read them. If you don't feel they are tense enough, you can simply tighten these muscles internally.

- **Arms**: Make fists and press your elbows back into the surface behind you or beneath you. Alternatively (or as well), you can press your elbows into your sides.
- **Face**: Furrow your brow as if confused, scrunch up your nose and cheeks, and press your teeth together lightly (don't clench). You can also press your tongue to the roof of your mouth.
- **Neck**: Bring your chin down toward your chest while pulling your neck back at the same time. It should feel as if the front and back of your neck are in a tug-of-war.
- **Torso**: Take a deep breath, high into your lungs, while simultaneously pulling your shoulders back and tightening your abdomen.
- **Legs and Feet**: Lift your legs while simultaneously pulling them in toward yourself. At the same time bend your ankles to bring your feet and toes back toward your shin.

Get ready to tense all the muscles in your body like a tin man. Tense them now. Feel the tension. Notice how the tension feels. Notice where all the tension is coming from. Hold the tension for about eight seconds. Releasing into scarecrow. Loose, soft, no joints. Noticing the difference between how your muscles feel now as compared to before [pause], limp and soft. No joints like a scarecrow. Making no effort to relax, just allowing your body to feel released, loose, soft, and relaxed. Enjoying the relaxation for 30–40 seconds and repeat the tin-man-to-scarecrow cycle one or two more times.

If you have more time, you can work through the muscle groups separately.

EXERCISE Differential Relaxation

1. Noticing how your book or device feels in your hands, staying in the same position while letting go of any tension you don't need. Allowing your muscles to be as loose and soft as they will be.

2. Move to a position such that you will have less tension. This includes putting down your book, perhaps leaning back against the surface beneath you or uncrossing your legs. Once you put the book down, allowing your muscles to be as loose and soft as they will be.

3. Put the book down and stand with the least amount of tension. Where do you need no tension at all while standing? You need no tension in your hands, arms, shoulders, and face. Letting go completely in those areas. Using the least amount everywhere else. You need the most tension in your legs, but, even in your legs, letting go of about half of the tension there. If you aren't swaying, letting go even more.

4. Soon I'm going to ask you to walk at your normal pace with the least amount of tension. When you do, let your arms swing freely with no tension in them or your face and shoulders. Put your book down and begin your walk now.

5. Next I will ask you to walk very fast as if you are in a big hurry, but without running. The only tension you will add is slightly more tension in your legs. Walk in this way now. What did you notice? Were you surprised at how little extra energy or tension you needed to walk very fast? Next time you are in a hurry, overwhelmed, or otherwise stressed, remember how little tension you needed to walk very fast. We often use way more tension than we need when we are running behind or feeling overwhelmed.

6. Put a question mark on several sticky notes. Put them in places you will see frequently and places that you associate with stress. When you see these reminders, think, "Do I need all this tension?" or "What's the least amount of tension I can use?" If you have more of a problem with fatigue than with tension, substitute the word "energy" for tension in the above sentences.

EXERCISE Cheap Biofeedback

Do you have tension in your face? When alone, driving, or with people with whom you're comfortable sharing your goals for being more relaxed, wear a piece of tape on your forehead. If you have bangs, you can wear the tape comfortably anywhere. If not, perhaps you can create bangs to hide your tape. You'll feel it when you raise your brows or furrow your brow and it will remind you to soften those areas.

Also, very inexpensive thermal biofeedback helps people to relax. Remember mood rings? Biodots or biosquares work the same way except you typically attach them to your fingertips. They cost less than $20 for 100 online. Aim to change the color by thinking of warming your fingertips. Autogenic training involves visualizing and imagining warming the fingers and arms, then eventually the feet and legs. It also includes imagining that they are heavy. This has been shown to be effective in increasing circulation and is particularly helpful in treating migraine headaches. It is suggested to learn this from a trained therapist, but imagining your hands and arms as being heavy and warm won't harm you.

EXERCISE Clouds (Optional Recording)

This next exercise is imagery of lying on a raft becoming progressively more and more relaxed with each passing cloud. If you happen to be afraid of water, visualize yourself on the sand or in a lounge chair.

Visualizing yourself lying on a large, dry air mattress. You can be in a deep or shallow pool, on a pond, or on a lake. It can be somewhere that you've been before, somewhere you've seen in a movie or a photo, or a place you make up in your imagination. Begin by feeling the warmth of the sun with a nice, gentle breeze [pause]. As you look up into the sky, it's mostly blue, but you're noticing a few white fluffy clouds floating across your field of vision [pause]. Noticing a cloud shaped like the number 9. As you watch it floating through the sky, you feel a little more relaxed [pause]. Noticing a cloud shaped like the number 8 moving across the sky and feeling more floaty [pause]. As you see the 7 drifting across the sky, feeling a sense of peace and tranquility [pause]. Watching the number 6 float across the sky as your sense of peace and tranquility doubles [pause]. Noticing your body sinking into the raft as you watch the cloud shaped like the number 5 drifting across the sky [pause]. Allowing your sense of floating to double as you watch the 4 following the 5 [pause]. Just watching the 3 and enjoying how you feel [pause]. Allowing the sense of sinking into the raft to double as you watch the 2 [pause]. Allowing the relaxation to double or becoming as relaxed as you'd like to be as you watch the 1 [pause]. Memorizing how you feel as you watch the cloud shaped like a zero move across the sky [pause].

EXERCISE Balloons (Optional Recording)

Use this exercise when you feel overwhelmed by your to-do list.

Visualizing that you are outdoors. This can be in your backyard, the park, or anywhere else outside. Imagining that you are holding a handful of helium balloons. Each balloon represents a different one of your tasks. Feeling a breeze on the back of your body. As you're holding this handful of balloons, thinking about what you are going to be doing after this [pause]. Taking the balloon that represents what you are doing next into your free hand. If the thing you're doing next is something you are looking forward to doing, make the balloon your favorite color. Letting go of the handful of balloons, watching them climb higher in the sky from the helium as the wind moves them farther and farther away. Seeing the balloons appearing smaller and smaller in your field of vision [pause]. Soon they are just a few little dots in the sky until they completely disappear. Focusing on your next event. If the balloon you're still holding is a task or worry, you're relaxing now, such that it is best to focus on the moment by letting go of this last balloon too. Watching it float up into the sky and drifting further away [pause]. Seeing it get smaller and smaller until it's just a dot in the sky before it disappears completely. When it disappears, focusing your attention on the moment, noticing the surfaces beneath you or switching to another relaxation strategy.

EXERCISE Brain Sink (Optional Recording)

Visualizing that you have a sink in your brain. Visualizing that your worries are moving around in that sink. Imagining that you pull out the plug and the words drain out of your head. If you'd like, you can turn on the water and use the spraying function to help wash the thoughts out of the sink.

| EXERCISE | Slowing Racing Thoughts With Imagery |

Nothing in nature goes from fast to stop in an instant. Therefore, when we have racing thoughts, trying to stop them with a relaxation strategy rarely works. As you will read in the next chapter, it is important to catch anxiety and worry early in the spiral to prevent it from getting out of control. However, this group of imagery exercises can help you to reverse your spiral. By meeting the racing thoughts where they are, you can gradually slow them before using another coping strategy, including any of the relaxation exercises in this chapter. Next time you have racing thoughts, try these exercises.

Playground Merry-Go-Round

1. Visualize the big spinning disc with railings that you see at playgrounds.
2. Visualize yourself holding onto a rail and running as fast as you can with your thoughts.
3. Then hop on and think of your thoughts gradually slowing as the merry-go-round slows.
4. When it has almost stopped, hop off and visualize the merry-go-round becoming more and more distant.
5. Shift to being in the moment or using another relaxation strategy.

Sprint to Walk

1. Visualize yourself sprinting as fast as you can with your thoughts.
2. Now run—still fast, but not as fast as you can. Slow your thoughts accordingly.
3. Take it down to a jog.
4. Next slow to a fast walk.
5. Shift to walking slowly.
6. Move to the moment or continue visualizing yourself on a walk enjoying the great outdoors.

Old-Time Record Player (Optional Recording)

This may not be helpful if you were born after CDs, MP3s, and streaming became the norm. The idea is to imagine your racing thoughts on a 45rpm record playing at 78. Then lowering the speed to 45 and lowering the volume. Lower the speed down to 33⅓ and turn the volume down gradually to off. Follow with a coping strategy of your choice. If you aren't familiar with these record players, think of thoughts recorded at a normal pace being played at a fast pace, then the pace at which they were recorded, and then slowly. Lower the volume with each slower speed.

13 Chapter | Nip the Worry Spiral in the Bud

Anxiety and worry occur in a spiral of interactions between thoughts, images, physical sensations, and behaviors. Not all people who worry excessively experience all of them, but each person experiences the spiral similarly each time. Often, we are not aware of our anxiety until it's out of control. By the time we recognize it, the anxiety is high and most of the strategies are useless. In fact, when they don't work, it can make things worse. When we try to manage worry and it doesn't work, it can lead to frustration and a feeling of helplessness that can contribute to depression.

The goal is to catch worry early when the anxiety is low and the strategies are more powerful against it. We regularly see this in medicine, where it's well known that catching everything from the common cold to cancer early in the process makes treatment easier and more successful. It's similar when it comes to preventing worry from getting out of control; an ounce of prevention is worth a pound of cure.

There are two ways in which you can prevent your worry—and thereby anxiety, depression, and frustration—from getting out of control. First is to use the strategies you have learned to nip your anxiety in the bud—that is, to catch the worry spiral before it gets out of control and apply the strategies you learned in the previous chapters. The second goal is to use your strategies throughout the day to prevent anxiety and worry from taking hold in the first place. When we are more relaxed, we are less apt to begin to worry.

Think about what causes you stress. What is associated with the beginning of your spirals or even instances where your anxiety spikes quickly? Some of the most common are family, to-do lists, emails, bills, and business calls. You want to think in two ways. The first is "What starts the spiral?" And the second is "What do you do in response to this spiral?" For instance, you sense that your son is out past curfew, you feel a pit in your stomach, and you check the time or maybe you text your son. Ideally, your realization that he is late is conscious and you use a coping strategy. However, we don't usually notice our spirals until they have gained some momentum. You probably won't even notice the pit in your stomach, yet. Therefore, it's important to set up reminders. For instance, if you change the wallpaper on your phone, when you next go to text your son, the new wallpaper can remind you to use your strategies, stressed or not.

Another very useful reminder is sticky notes. Put them both in places that you associate with stress (to catch anxiety early) and in places where you will see them frequently (to help you maintain relaxation, making it less likely that spirals will start). Similarly, you can put a colorful rubber band, hair band, or twisty tie around something that you use frequently.

The next page has several suggestions that you can circle and also write in your own reminders.

Creating Reminders to
Use Coping Strategies

CHANGE THINGS ON YOUR DEVICES (e.g., Smartphone, Tablet, Computer)

Circle the reminders you'd like to have. If you can, take time now to make these changes.

Wallpaper	*Ring tone*
Text tone	*Email tone*
Email notification	*Use the MindBell (or similar) app*
Add a small sticker	

PUT UP STICKY NOTES

Considering places you will see frequently and places associated with stress, circle the places you'd like to have sticky note reminders. If you can, take time to place these now.

Dash of car	*Refrigerator*
Light switches	*Faucets*
Computer (especially where email notifications pop up)	*TV*
Doorframes	*Pantry*
Mirrors	*Clocks*
Remote control	*Notebooks*
Books (especially textbooks or training manuals)	*Planners*

ADD A HAIRBAND, COLORFUL RUBBER BAND, OR TWISTY TIE

Place one or more of these reminders around the following things. Circle the ones you'd like to use and consider adding these reminders now.

Mug	*Water bottle*
Cup	*Soda can*
Key ring (or even change your key ring)	*Smartphone*
Wrist	

After about two weeks, you won't notice your reminders as much. Therefore, change your reminders regularly (e.g., change the color of your sticky notes, write something on your sticky notes, or change aspects of your phone). The goal is to use the coping strategies from previous chapters without stopping your flow of activity so that it is not inconvenient to practice them as many as 50 times per day or more. If you have extra time and you'd like to stop for several seconds or a few minutes to practice the strategies in more depth, of course that's fine. In addition to changing devices, sticky notes, or hairbands, feel free to use your own reminders, including when you begin to feel anxious. You can also ask others who witness your nervous habits to gently remind you to engage in a strategy.

Change the "Applying Strategies?" column of your daily monitoring (see the worksheet "Daily Self-Monitoring 2" in Chapter 11). Instead of using the rating scale, estimate the number of times you applied your strategies. If your anxiety is low and your use of strategies is low, that's alright. If your anxiety is moderate or high and your application of strategies is infrequent (less than 20 times), use the monitoring as a motivator to create new reminders or change your current reminders, as well as to apply the strategies rather than ignoring the reminders. Remember you can apply these strategies without taking any extra time. If you stop each time you see a reminder, you will get frustrated.

Use situations in which you are waiting as an opportunity to practice your strategies. Whether you're waiting in line, for an appointment, or for a friend, rather than using your smartphone or tablet, use at least part of the time to practice your strategies. Just missed a red light? Reframe it as an opportunity to apply your strategies. Running late? The strategies might be even more useful.

Once you get into the habit of catching anxiety and using your coping strategies, begin to use stressors as a reminder. When you see your boss walking toward you, use your strategies before a conversation begins. If you see that a difficult relative is calling, letting go of any tension before you answer the phone. Put a sticky note on your computer where you receive email alerts.

14 | Positive Psychology
Chapter

Positive psychology is much more than positive thinking. It is the study of what makes people happy. Obviously, happy people are not going to be depressed and are less likely to feel very anxious. Certainly, even very well adjusted people will feel sad when they lose a friend, family member, or pet and they will feel anxious in dangerous situations. However, they are likely to recover from these events more quickly and easily.

Positive psychology focuses not on reducing depression and anxiety but on increasing happiness and peace. Therefore, this chapter can be helpful even if you do not suffer from depression.

In Chapter 2, we discussed moving toward relaxation rather than fighting anxiety (remember the blue monkeys). Here, we move toward happiness rather than fighting depression. One way to do this is to list gratitudes—that is, what you are grateful for. If you tend to be a negative thinker, you might find yourself focusing on what you don't like in your life rather than looking at what you have and what is good about your life. Perhaps you're not particularly negative but you take your blessings for granted. One of the many goals of positive psychology is to be more mindful of what you are grateful for in your life on a daily basis. While some negative thoughts are sure to peek through, let them be brief thoughts, and even try to see the up-side to a negative situation.

EXERCISE Smile

Smile, laugh, and sing more and you'll feel better about life. Sound simple? It is!

Make a big smile while noticing how it feels. Now frown. Smile again. Feel the difference?

What did you experience?

Take it a step further and laugh even though nothing is funny. How does it feel?

Put up yellow sticky notes in your home, car, and office. When you notice them, smile even if you don't feel like it.

Gratitudes

1. What are the things that you are grateful for about yourself? First, consider internal factors, such as: good sense of humor, intelligent, friendly, athletic, creative, high energy, patient, loyal, or reliable, just to name a few. In other words, what attributes do you have that you like? Put these in positive terms (e.g., "I'm smart" or "I have above-average intelligence" vs. "I'm not stupid"). Aim for 10 things, but find at least five:

   If you couldn't come up with at least five, think about positive things that others have said about you, compliments you've received, or times you felt good about yourself and why. Consider asking a friend or family member what they think. Write it down even if you think it's only a bit true.

   _____   _____

   _____   _____

   _____   _____

   _____   _____

2. Now what are the external factors you like about yourself? These are physical attributes, such as: full head of hair, nice legs, pretty eyes, height, slenderness, muscularity, great eyesight, or straight teeth. If you are shy about listing these positive attributes, add compliments you've received from others. Aim for six, but find at least three:

   _____   _____

   _____   _____

   _____   _____

   If you couldn't come up with at least three, get help from a friend or family member.

3. Who are the people in your life you are grateful to have? Think about family, friends, neighbors, co-workers, a good therapist, a doctor, or a house cleaner. You can even be grateful for someone you had in the past who was a positive influence in your life, such as a teacher, coach, or grandparent. List as many as you can. Five is good, but aim for more than 10, even 20 if you can. (Hopefully this exercise will lead to positive emotions. If it doesn't, work on a plan to meet more people or become more connected with people you don't know well. It may be wise to see a therapist to help you with this.)

   _____   _____

   _____   _____

   _____   _____

_____ _____

_____ _____

_____ _____

_____ _____

_____ _____

_____ _____

4. What is it that you like about your major roles in life (e.g., job, parent, friend, caregiver)?

_____

_____

_____

_____

_____

5. Now think about the past 24 hours (or if it's late, you can just think about today). What are you grateful for about today? Come up with at least three things:

_____ _____

_____ _____

_____ _____

6. Over the next three weeks, come up with three things that you are grateful for each day. These can be constants in your life (e.g., my car, my daughter, my job, my health, my sense of humor) or they can be things that happened that day (e.g., the weather was great, I had a great laugh with my co-worker, I found a bargain on shoes). These can be things that you listed in 1–5, but do not repeat any of them over the next 21 days. Write these gratitudes on a separate piece of paper.

Mark these pages to return to them later. Read them daily, weekly, or just when you feel you'd benefit from the reminder. Consider continuing writing down three gratitudes per day on a regular basis. Or consider continuing them without writing them down (e.g., say them aloud or think of them on your commute).

If you have family dinners, consider asking each person to share their gratitudes at each evening meal.

Even though it first aired in 1951, most people have seen the Vitameatavegamin skit with Lucille Ball ("Lucy"). Lucy is hired to do a commercial for a liquid supplement called Vitameatavegamin. In the first take, she can't hide her disgust with the taste. She then stumbles over the words and makes various mistakes. Vitameatavegamin has alcohol in it, so with each subsequent take, she gets progressively more intoxicated, and it is hilarious! If you haven't seen it, find it online and watch it. Otherwise think of one of the funniest things that you've witnessed in your personal life or in a movie or TV show. As you think about this, notice your mood lifting.

EXERCISE **Favorite Funnies**

Below list three of your favorite "funnies," whether from your own life or from TV or movies:

1. _____

2. _____

3. _____

When you begin to feel depressed, anxious, or irritated, bring one of these funny memories or skits to mind.

EXERCISE **Dry Bathtub**

Do you sometimes realize that your worry is a little ridiculous? Next time, consider actually getting into a dry bathtub fully clothed to match your thoughts. Worry in the tub, laugh in the tub, then, when you feel better, get out.

EXERCISE **Embellish It!**

Take your worry to a ridiculous extreme. For instance, you're worried about being late to a party. Imagine that when you walk in there's a dead silence. Everyone stares at you. Then they start laughing and talk about your most embarrassing moments. The host tells you that you're too late and you need to go home. They throw tomatoes at you on the way out. For a very creative example of taking worry to a ridiculous extreme in the film *Amélie* (2001), go to YouTube and enter "Nino is Late."

Be Kind & Feel Better

There's a saying that when you are feeling most depressed, do something kind for someone else. Why wait until you're depressed? Choose a day to do all of the following. Write down what you did and how it made you feel.

1. Compliment at least two people on something physical—their hair, their jewelry, their clothing, etc.

   _____

   _____

2. Compliment at least two people on their positive attributes. Some examples are: "You are one of the kindest people I know," "I love your sense of humor," and "I admire your problem-solving abilities."

   _____

   _____

3. Do at least two kind things for at least two people. This could be as simple as opening the door for someone. It might be letting someone go in front of you in line. It could be helping a sick friend. Or it might be doing some volunteer work. Maybe it's even buying coffee for the stranger in line behind you.

   _____

   _____

4. Take the time to phone or email someone to let them know that something they did for you in the past really mattered to you.

   _____

   _____

5. Close your eyes and wish the best for yourself, for a stranger (nearby or someone in the news), for someone you love, and even for someone you don't really like.

   _____

   _____

You've probably heard someone say, "There's a yin and a yang to everything." Yin and yang are derived from ancient China and symbolize distinct but complementary forces—for instance, black and white, life and death, or good and evil. The yin is the dark side, so to speak, and the yang is the bright side. In the following worksheet, list things in your life that are currently stressful, sad, or otherwise troubling. These could be things that happened today or things that are ongoing. Once you have completed this list, write the upside, or Yang for each Yin. Some examples are:

Yin	Yang
Traffic was unusually bad today.	The sunset was gorgeous. I got a chance to listen to some great music.
My daughter's teacher was inappropriate.	I'm glad my daughter and I have the kind of relationship that she was able to tell me about it.
Strep throat is painful.	It's good to not have to work for a change. I'm enjoying the movies.
I'm so sad that my uncle died.	He lived a long, happy life. I'm grateful we were close.
My roof is leaking.	I'm lucky to have a home. I'm glad insurance will cover most of it.
I'm scared of the political climate.	I've bonded with friends with similar views. I haven't been directly affected yet.

Yin and Yang

For each troubling situation in your life today or ongoing (yin), list one to three related upsides or things for which you're grateful (yang).

Yin	Yang

EXERCISE   # Rain and Sunshine

Think for a moment about rain and sunshine. It's a fact that the happiest people are not people who have lived easy lives. The happiest are people who have lived through adversity. Some of this may be because we learn then what is most important. Living through adversity certainly can make us stronger. Finally, we appreciate the good times much more when we've been through bad times. We all enjoy a warm, sunny day much more if it was preceded by five rainy, cold, cloudy days than if it was preceded by 10 days of sunshine.

When you are going through tough times, remind yourself that there will be better times ahead. While you are going through good times, be present and enjoy them. While it's okay to know that there will certainly be some tough times ahead, so that you're not too frustrated, know that those tough times will be temporary too.

15 | Removing the Crutches
Chapter

It's good to have supportive friends and healthy, relaxing, and fun habits to get you through tough times and add a dimension to your life. It's also natural to find distractions that help you to temporarily forget the problems in your life. It's also okay to enjoy a drink at the end of the day if you don't have a history of addiction. However, sometimes the things that people do to cope with depression and anxiety feel good in the short term, but cause more problems with depression and anxiety in the long run.

The bottom line: there are healthy ways to cope and unhealthy ways to cope. Exercise is a particularly healthy way to cope. It often improves sleep and it keeps you in good physical condition. Moreover, the mental health benefits are undeniable. It increases the neurotransmitters serotonin and norepinephrine. Low levels of which are associated with depression and anxiety. In fact, the most commonly prescribed antidepressants (which can also be prescribed for the treatment of anxiety) artificially increase these neurotransmitters. Specifically, by blocking the re-uptake of serotonin and norepinephrine in the cells, they allow more of these beneficial substances to circulate in the brain, increasing our levels of them. Exercise increases our levels of these neurotransmitters naturally and directly—it is therefore a natural antidepressant and a natural anti-anxiety approach. Exercise also stimulates dopamine, which makes us feel happy. Weight training not only makes us stronger physically, it makes us feel stronger emotionally as well. Other positive habits that can be used to manage anxiety and depression that are not otherwise mentioned in this book are activities such as a date night, finding time to read a book or watch a movie, a massage, and socializing (unless it involves unhealthy amounts of alcohol or any intake of drugs).

Unhealthy ways to cope, or crutches, can be placed into two categories. The first category is habits that negatively reinforce bad habits. The second is unhealthy habits that both negatively and positively reinforce bad habits.

The terms "positive reinforcement" and "negative reinforcement" are typically misunderstood. To clarify, operant conditioning refers to behaviors that are either increased (reinforced) or decreased (punished) by adding a stimulus (positive) or removing a stimulus (negative). There is a great deal of confusion about positive reinforcement and negative reinforcement because people erroneously believe that "positive" means "good" and "negative" means "bad." This is *not* the case. Rather, "positive" means that we are *adding* something to *increase or decrease* the behavior. "Negative" means that we are *subtracting* or taking away something to *increase or decrease* the behavior.

Punishment occurs when a behavior has decreased. Reinforcement occurs when a behavior has increased. If we add something that decreases a behavior, that's positive punishment (e.g., a child has to do a chore for misbehaving and it decreases that behavior). If we subtract something that decreases the behavior, that's negative punishment (e.g., a child stops misbehaving after TV is taken away). If we add something and it increases a behavior, that behavior was positively reinforced (e.g., a child is praised for helping and they help more). A behavior is negatively reinforced when we take away or reduce something undesirable, such as anxiety, pain, or depression. For example, consider what happens if someone has a headache, takes an aspirin, the headache goes away, and they increase their use of aspirin when in pain: in this case, the act of taking an aspirin is negatively reinforced. It's reinforcing because the behavior of taking the aspirin is increased, but it is *negatively* reinforcing because the pain is taken away or reduced.

If you have a crutch associated with anxiety or depression, negative reinforcement is likely involved. Unfortunately, in the case of negative reinforcement, not only do the behaviors increase but anxiety and depression typically increase as well.

	Apply a Stimulus (+)	**Remove a Stimulus (−)**
Increases Behavior	*Positive Reinforcement* Erin studies more after getting $100 for each A.	*Negative Reinforcement* Bill keeps taking aspirin for his headache after he finds that it reduces his pain.
Decreases Behavior	*Positive Punishment* Andrew stops antagonizing Mason after his mom makes him clean Mason's room	*Negative Punishment* Jolene stops texting and driving when her parents take away her phone for two weeks for catching her texting and driving.

If someone takes an opiate for pain, the behavior can be both negatively and positively reinforced. Because it reduces or eliminates the pain, it's likely to negatively reinforce taking the drug. And, because it boosts mood, it can also be positively reinforcing. Finally, there can be additional negative reinforcement from a temporary reduction of depression or anxiety.

For the most part, those behaviors that positively and negatively reinforce anxiety to the point of it being problematic involve addictions, or substance abuse. If you have a glass of wine with dinner and it makes you feel good and you are more relaxed, this is not a problem. Everything in moderation. Overeating once a week or so also is not typically a problem. However, excessive use of alcohol or of prescription or illicit drugs; over-engagement in sex or pornography; excessive gambling; and overeating can be problematic when they become habits used to cope with anxiety or depression (e.g., missing work, driving under the influence, or hurting someone). These are serious issues and beyond the scope of this book. If any of these apply to you, it is recommended that you see a therapist who specializes in addictions, or at least go to Alcoholics Anonymous, Gamblers Anonymous, Overeaters Anonymous, or a similar group. If you have a therapist and you're hiding any of these crutch behaviors, I urge you to discuss them at your next session.

Until you resolve this issue, you will likely continue to suffer from the other problems that led you to open this book. In fact, if you have found the exercises and worksheets to be minimally effective or ineffective and are engaged in such addictive behaviors, it is probably because you are relying on your addiction instead of relying on the principles in this book. Similarly, if you are using a class of drugs known as benzodiazepines (e.g., clonazepam/ Klonopin, alprazolam/Xanax, lorazepam/Ativan, or diazepam/Valium) and are not improving or are feel stuck, it's best to work with your prescribing doctor to gradually reduce your reliance on these medications. Please note that suddenly stopping using alcohol, benzodiazepines, opiates, and other addictive drugs is potentially dangerous. So please consult your physician about a plan to gradually decrease them while increasing reliance on the strategies in the book, preferably with the help of a therapist.

Hopefully, if you have crutches, they are limited to the negatively-reinforcing kind that don't involve drugs, alcohol, or other addictive behaviors. Negative reinforcement is particularly problematic in obsessive–compulsive disorder and phobias. However, it can be a problem with any anxiety issue. The frustrating fact is that many of the things people do to try to make their anxiety better usually help in the short term, but make the anxiety worse (or at least serve to maintain it) in the long run. Technically, these are negatively-reinforcing behaviors, but we can just call them crutches.

Examples of crutches include calling a loved one to make sure they are okay when it isn't necessary, repetitively seeking reassurance that goes beyond advice, keeping Xanax in your purse or wallet "just in case," repeatedly reassuring yourself such that you "see-saw" or "ping-pong" in your mind (worry, reassuring thought, worry, reassuring thought, etc.), frequently checking your heart rate or blood pressure (or other medical information), and avoiding situations because of worry or fear about what might happen. All these crutches either make you feel better or avoid increasing your fear in the short term. In turn, this maintains or increases these behaviors while increasing the accompanying anxiety such that it is threatening to think of removing, or even reducing, your crutches. In some cases, just removing these crutches will be very helpful. However, it may also be necessary to take some steps to directly face your fears.

An example is someone we'll call Henry. Henry is worried that there is something wrong with his heart even though he's seen a cardiologist who cleared him. He checks his heart rate with a heart rate app as many as 25 times per day (this is crutch one). And he has purchased two blood-pressure machines so he can check his blood pressure both at home and at work, and he checks it at least 10 times per day, often more (this is crutch two).

There are several ways Henry could approach his problem. He could try to stop using both crutches at the same time, wean himself off both, or address each crutch separately by either weaning or stopping "cold turkey." I might recommend that he begin by checking his heart rate and blood pressure only upon rising, at meal times, and at bedtime. Once he begins to get relatively comfortable with this, he could reduce his checks to just one of those times, and then finally stop completely or check his vitals only once per week.

If Henry were avoiding exercising out of fear of a cardiac event, he could sprint to face his fear. Alternatively, he could return to the exercise program he used before his worry got out of control, or gradually work his way up to his old routine. Use the following sheets to make a plan for reducing your crutches and monitor your progress to keep up your motivation.

Identify + Plan
to Manage Crutches

List habits in your life that you believe are crutches, including addictive behaviors.

1. _____

2. _____

3. _____

4. _____

5. _____

If applicable, circle what you plan to quit completely right now.

For any crutches remaining, decide how frequently you want to use them in the period before you quit or possibly reduce them to a healthy level. Below, write your plan for each crutch.

_____

_____

_____

_____

_____

_____

Reduce/Manage Crutches

Use this monitoring form to track your progress while beginning to rely more on the strategies in this workbook and other strategies your therapist has suggested.

Date	Crutch	Planned Number of Times Used or Time Spent	Actual Number of Times Used or Time Spent	Anxiety Rating (0–10)

16 Chapter | The "P" Sheet: Preferred Ways to Think Instead of Worrying

After several years of specializing in treating worry, I realized that many of the strategies I teach start with the letter "P":

- **Prevent** anxiety from getting out of control by catching it early.
- **Postpone** worries to another time.
- **Problem-solve** your concerns instead of worrying about them.
- **Process words** are gentler and thereby more effective than commands when moving toward relaxation.
- Focus on the **Present** because worry is about the future. Focusing on our senses puts us in the moment.

Two additional strategies covered in this workbook have been changed to "P" words. These are:

- **Permitting** thoughts and feelings. This is another way to say "mindful acceptance."
- **Positive thoughts** include both B³s and being mindful of what you are grateful for.

Finally, it occurred to me that two other types of thinking that start with the letter "P" are ways of thinking that are preferred to worry. While much more than a way of thinking to many, praying is better than worrying. Prayer translates worries into a request for help so that we are essentially doing something about it, as well as adding the additional benefit of faith. In fact, when things that we worry about are out of control, many people are comforted by saying or thinking, "I'm giving it over to God," so as to reach acceptance of the outcome and let go of worry. This is similar to acceptance; you are trusting that God will take over. A popular serenity prayer includes both acceptance and problem-solving:

> *God, grant me the serenity to accept the things I cannot change,*
>
> *Courage to change the things I can,*
>
> *And wisdom to know the difference.*

Regardless of your religious beliefs, these are healthy words to live by. In addition, if you feel overwhelmed by changing the things you want to change, consider accepting the things you aren't ready to change yet. This can be very helpful too.

Another "P" word is "pleasant." Mindfulness and "being in the now" have become increasingly popular over the past couple of decades. The emphasis in the media and in books on being in the moment may have given thoughts about the past and the future a bad name. It's true that being in the moment frees us from depressing regrets from the past and worry about the future. However, it's very healthy to reflect on warm and happy memories from the past and to fantasize, or look forward to, events in the future. Therefore, thinking pleasant thoughts is a preferred way of thinking.

Finally, it's necessary to do some planning in life, and this is better than worrying. While planning is similar to problem-solving, it is different because we can spend a lot of time planning when there are no actual problems to be solved. For example, scheduling a vacation, organizing a birthday party, and even making a to-do list are planning and can be done without worry. Perhaps planning can even prevent worry.

Therefore, we can add three more styles of thinking that are better than worrying:

- **Prayer**, especially giving worries over to God, the universe, or a higher power.
- **Pleasant thoughts**, which can include warm and happy memories of the past, fantasies, and looking forward to events in the future.
- **Planning** is a necessary part of thinking that need not involve anxiety.

Hopefully, you'll get into the habit of using the following form indefinitely. After all, it only takes about a minute to do. However, it is human nature that once we are feeling better about a problem we've taken measures to correct, we slack off and even stop practicing our healthy patterns. Without the discomfort, we may even forget to use our strategies.

Whether it's doing physical therapy, eating well, prioritizing sleep, or managing anxiety and depression, after stopping our healthy habits, the problems tend to sneak back up. Sometimes, nipping anxiety in the bud, using B^{3}s, being grateful, and using some of the other strategies become habits and are automatic. However, during more stressful times, the old habits sometimes rear their ugly heads. So try to remember that if and when you start to feel depressed or anxious in the future, you can go back to using this sheet before the problems get out of control.

Monitoring Daily Preferred "Ps"

This monitoring form is designed to keep you mindful of engaging in these strategies on a regular basis. Positive thoughts are divided into two categories, gratefulness and B³s. Feel free to cross off any strategies that you do not find helpful. In the boxes, you have a choice. You can just check the box if you applied the strategy and mark an X or a dash if you didn't. Alternatively, you may record an estimate of how many times you applied it, give yourself a letter grade, or rate it on a numbered scale (e.g., 1–10).

	Mon	Tues	Wed	Thurs	Fri	Sat	Sun
Prevent							
Postpone							
Problem-solve							
Process words							
Present focus							
Permitting (accepting)							
Positive thoughts I: Gratefulness							
Positive thoughts II: B³s							
Prayer							
Pleasant thoughts							
Planning							

17 | Getting Motivated
Chapter | to Manage Depression

Low motivation is one of many symptoms of depression. Often a vicious cycle, it is frequently the most problematic symptom of depression because it can cause you to get behind with tasks and activities, isolate you from people, cause you to avoid doing things you used to enjoy, and even cause you to avoid self-care. After weeks or months of falling further and further behind, your to-do list can seem insurmountable, making it even more difficult to get started. Often these tasks create anxiety and not only pile on responsibility, but also pile on more depression. Furthermore, you get out of practice with doing things that used to bring you pleasure, such as engaging in hobbies and spending time with friends. Watching TV, eating poorly, isolating, and the like become the new normal.

Perhaps the most difficult obstacle about having a lack of motivation is that it is difficult to get motivated to do things that will help you get better. However, the fact that you are reading this is a very good sign that you have at least *some* motivation. Even though it may be a bit overwhelming, make a list of the things you used to do that you wish you had the motivation to do now. While making the list, keep in mind that you don't have to do any of these things today. This may include exercise, socializing, housekeeping, ways of dressing, hygiene habits, or engaging in a hobby. It may also include tasks such as paying bills or maintaining your car or house.

My List

_____   _____   _____

_____   _____   _____

_____   _____   _____

_____   _____   _____

_____   _____   _____

You probably feel a bit overwhelmed from making that list. Thinking about finding the energy to get back to your prime and do these things can be so overwhelming that it can zap your energy and ultimately even leave you immobile. The most important thing to remember to prevent yourself from feeling too overwhelmed is to take one step at a time.

Shortly, I will ask you to choose one thing to work on. Before you do that, consider that feeling of being on the fence about socializing, exercising, or having sex. Usually when people who are mildly to moderately depressed decide to go out with friends, ride their bike, go for a walk, or make love, they are almost always glad later that they did it and usually enjoy it more than they had predicted. Has this happened to you?

Write down two instances when you engaged in an activity that you almost chose not to do because your motivation or desire to do it was low?

_____

_____

How did you feel while you were doing them?

_____

How did you feel after you did them?

_____

Have there been instances when you have done one of these things and you were sorry you did it?

_____

When you had been on the fence, what percentage of time have you been glad that you did the activity?

_____%

Before you decide what to do first, how many of the items on your list do you think you might enjoy once you start doing them? Put a check mark next to them.

Now underline the items on the list that you think there is a greater than 50% chance will make you feel better once you have made some progress on them or have accomplished the task.

Now circle just one of the things above that you want to do first. If in doubt, pick one that you both checked and underlined. Alternatively, choose the thing that involves the least effort. Indecisiveness is also common with depression. If you can't decide, definitely choose physical exercise, or, if that is not on your list, choose to socialize. Otherwise choose the first item you circled.

If you chose exercise and you haven't been doing it lately, do not expect to run six miles or spend an hour at the gym. Instead, start with something like a 15–20-minute walk or plan to stay at the gym for 20–30 minutes. Once you're engaged, you may find you stop after you've hit your initial 15–30-minute goal. That's fine! Give yourself credit for getting started. However, you may also find that, once you get started, you want to keep going. By all means, do so. And if 15 minutes seems too long, any exercise is a start and better than nothing!

Consider involving a walking or workout buddy. Or find someone who will play tennis with you or go in-line skating. If you make a commitment to go with someone, you'll be more likely to exercise and then you will be socializing at the same time. It's a win–win! Don't have anyone? Check online to see whether there is a group in your area for an activity that you enjoy.

Socialization is a major part of what brings us happiness. To start, it's probably best to socialize with people who are positive, funny, warm, and supportive. Remember misery loves company, so, because you don't want to remain miserable, avoid being with people who are likely to bring you down. Also, consider what is easiest. For example, if you sometimes meet with friends for coffee nearby and it's casual, that will be easier than planning a dinner with friends who dress up and tend to meet at a less convenient place. For making social plans, "When in doubt, get out!" can be a useful phrase to remember. If you have no one to socialize with, it is recommended that you see a therapist to help you develop strategies to meet new people and rekindle old friendships, and that will also give you one more person to talk to.

Rather than forcing yourself to do these things, I encourage you to think of it as an experiment. Give these strategies a try to see what happens. If you never exercise and don't particularly enjoy it, I still encourage you to walk or start another exercise program that seems least difficult. Our bodies are meant to move. Unfortunately, modern conveniences and the computer age have led us to be increasingly sedentary, and that certainly contributes to depression and anxiety!

Write down the one thing that you are choosing to do (see Happy You Did It? worksheet):

_____

If you have time to do this thing and it's a solitary activity, put down your book and do it now. Otherwise, schedule it by writing it in your calendar. If it involves another person, contact that person, or people, to schedule it.

If your activity involves others, pick a back-up activity in the event that you have difficulty scheduling, If you're motivated do both!

Once you have done the activity, use the Satisfaction Rating Scale to indicate how much you enjoyed it.

Satisfaction Rating Scale

Rate your level of enjoyment, or how glad you are that you did the activity:

0	1	2	3	4	5
No enjoyment	Almost no enjoyment	OK, but wish I hadn't done it	Some enjoyment; glad I did it	Enjoyed it; glad I did it	Really enjoyed it; very glad I did it

In the days to come, pick at least one activity per day. If you don't actually do it, that's alright. Just consider the possibility of engaging in an enjoyable activity daily. Don't set your expectations too high. In fact, if you haven't engaged in any pleasurable activities for several weeks, even following through with one thing a week is a good start. For each thing that you ponder doing, use the Motivation and Satisfaction Monitoring Form on the next page, as well as the Satisfaction Rating Scale in the previous exercise.

This is a monitoring sheet for exercise, socialization, and sex. If you do not have a partner or you have never really enjoyed sex, you can skip this part and focus on socializing and exercise. You could also add a hobby in place of sex on the monitoring form. Or, if you are already regularly engaging in exercise, social events, and/or sex, you could add hobbies in place of the things you don't feel you need help motivating yourself to do. Exercise, social events, sex, and engaging in a hobby are likely to help you feel better even when you don't feel motivated to do them.

Once you have started getting back into activities that give you pleasure, you can begin to tackle chores or tasks that you want to get crossed off your list, or maybe there are things you want to start doing again, such as cooking. Think about a way to ease into it. For example, if you used to make breakfast daily and want to get back into making breakfast again, start by making toast for a few days, then make toast and eggs, and next you can add bacon.

Remember that "inch by inch it's a cinch" but "yard by yard it's hard." Enacting this plan means to either divide activities into small, easily doable tasks or decide to commit to small time frames. For example, if you are behind on your mail, you could either commit to a small stack (perhaps a quarter or a third of your mail pile) or take 15 minutes to go through your mail. For more information, go to the second half of Chapter 22, on procrastination.

If you found that, most of the time, when you were on the fence about socializing or engaging in something else, you did it, and you enjoyed it, remember that. The next time you are in doubt, go out or otherwise engage. If you are still really struggling with depression and unable to get motivated, your therapist may recommend medication or various alternative approaches. If you aren't seeing a therapist, you may want to find one, consider medication, or at least look at Therapist Chapter 17 and Therapist Chapter 24.

The remaining chapters are optional. It is unlikely that they all apply to you. The title of each chapter may be enough for you to decide whether it applies to you. If not, the questions at the beginning of the chapters or the first paragraph will help you decide which ones are worth reading.

Motivation and
Satisfaction Monitoring

This form is for monitoring your motivation and satisfaction for exercise, socialization, and sex.

Rate your motivation on a 0–5 scale as follows:

0	1	2	3	4	5
Can't do it	Not motivated; would really have to force myself	Easier not to do it	On the fence	Know I'll feel better so I'll do it	Want to do it

	SOCIAL EVENT		EXERCISE		SEX	
Date	Motivation	Satisfaction	Motivation	Satisfaction	Motivation	Satisfaction
1/15	Dinner with Lucy: 2	4	20 min walk: 1	3	2	4

18 | Liberate Yourself:
Chapter | Say "No"

Do you find it difficult to say "no"?

Do you feel guilty when you put yourself first?

Do you rarely, if ever, ask others for help or support?

Do you do a lot of things in life because you feel like you "should" but you don't really want to do it?

If you answered "yes" to some of these questions, learning to say "no" may help your depression and anxiety. A significant contributor to many individuals' depression and anxiety is a habit of consistently putting others (e.g., family, work, and friends) ahead of themselves. Some people have this habit in all areas of their lives, even with strangers, while others may only have difficulty saying "no" in one area of their lives. When you put others' needs ahead of your own time after time, you may feel good about yourself for being so helpful. You may like that you consider yourself to be a good person because you put others ahead of yourself. You might be *motivated* by guilt and fear, but you rarely if ever *feel* guilty or fearful, because you keep on giving.

Despite feeling good about yourself in some ways, it is also very likely that you will feel devalued and unsupported. Because your needs aren't being met, you're left feeling depressed. Rushing to meet the demands of others while attempting to meet your own needs can leave you feeling stressed, overwhelmed, exhausted, or all three. If you feel well balanced in what you give and get from work, friends, and family, then you may skip this chapter. If you believe you give more than you get in return or that your habit of taking care of others is responsible for some of your own problems, continue.

If you have difficulty saying "no," practice with your therapist or supportive friend or relative. Consider reading *The Assertive Option* (Jakubowski & Lange, 1978), *When I Say No, I Feel Guilty* (Smith, 1985), or another book your therapist recommends. However, you can begin to practice saying "no" in the mirror right away. Below are some sample phrases of what you can say:

1. I'm sorry, I'm not going to be able to help you out this time.
2. I'm sorry, I have a policy to not lend money to anyone.
3. I have other plans. (Your plans may be a commitment to clean your house, to stay home and read, to go the gym, or to spend time with your family. This is truthful. You do not need to have a specific commitment in order to say "no.")
4. I'm not sure whether I'm going to be able to help you. Let me check my schedule and get back to you.
5. I'd like to be able to help you move for a couple hours in the afternoon. (When requested all day.) I'll text you before 1 o'clock to see where you are.
6. I won't be able to keep Kyle and Kaycee all weekend, but I'd be happy to watch them on Sunday.
7. From now on I'm only going to be able to come over and help you once a week.

Give and Take

Make a list below of people to whom you give more than you receive. The thing you give can be anything from listening to friends' problems to running errands to spending time with a sick or elderly person. Include in the list things that you have volunteered to do that are not 100% necessary or that you feel are necessary only because you made a commitment and you honor them. This list may include doing things at work that are outside your job, being on boards, taking care of neighbors, volunteer work, or helping at your kids' schools. Next to each item on the list, write what you do for the person or organization that isn't truly your responsibility, regardless of the degree to which you want to do the thing or feel obliged to do it.

_____   _____

_____   _____

_____   _____

_____   _____

_____   _____

_____   _____

List people who do more for you than you do for them.

_____   _____

_____   _____

List the people who are fairly equal. That is, your relationship is a give and take.

_____   _____

_____   _____

What did you learn by making these three lists?

_____

_____

On the one hand, the world is a better place because people help each other and because we have volunteers and good samaritans. On the other hand, some people lead unhappy and stressful lives from repeatedly giving time after time, especially when they get little support from others. Keeping this in mind, circle the things that you are clear you enjoy doing and that you want to continue to do. Continue doing these things with joy!

Now draw a line through the things that you do out of guilt or fear. What will be the advantages of saying "no" to these things? List the advantages below:

_____   _____

_____   _____

_____   _____

Do an experiment. Stop doing the items you crossed off. Or at least try not doing them for one week and see how it feels. If you aren't willing to do a week, think about how long you would be willing to run this experiment. Use acceptance strategies (see Chapter 3) to deal with the uncomfortable feelings and use B³s (see Chapter 8) to remind yourself that it's not your responsibility. Enjoy the advantages of not doing these things.

Some things we do partly because we want to and partly out of duty. For those items, take a moment to think about how you could change the situation so that the thing is something you do more because you want to. In the list on page 89, items 5, 6, and 7 are examples of these assertive compromises. Keep practicing saying these things until they become more comfortable, or at least much less uncomfortable. Remember too that your needs matter and it's important for your mental health to put yourself first much of the time.

An example that many baby boomers are facing is helping elderly parents; many millennials help their grandparents. Let's say you visit them three to four times a week for many hours. You are certain that you want to spend time with them and help them, but it's taking a toll on your social life and your own home, maybe even your work. Perhaps you want to make them the priority once or twice a week and make your life the priority on all other days. Only go over more than that if you really want to and you have extra time, or if there is an urgent situation. Perhaps you can make more of an effort to spend shorter periods of quality time together rather than just logging large numbers of hours?

People may catch you off guard, leading you to say "yes." Before you know it, you've made a commitment to something you don't want to do. It isn't good to say "yes" and then change your mind to "no" unless something unexpected comes up. It's much better to say "no" or "probably not" and then reconsider. Item 4 on page 89 is an example of not committing. It's a good exercise to get into the habit of saying you're not sure unless you are absolutely certain you want to. In fact, it's a good idea to practice saying "no" initially. You can always change your mind after saying "no."

This next form aims to help you to be more aware of what you give that you want to give and what you give out of guilt and fear. It is also a reminder of your choices. Use this monitoring form on a daily basis until you feel you are saying "yes" only when you want to say "yes" and making comprises that you want to do. Hopefully, you will enjoy doing the things that you want to do for people even more, and most importantly, feel less depressed and less overwhelmed as you start to reclaim your time to take care of yourself and to do the things that are most important in your life.

Giving, Receiving, & Saying "No"

This form can help to motivate you to keep track of your self-sacrificing and assertive behaviors. Write numbers in the spaces below unless a column is not applicable, in which case put "n/a."

Date	Hours spent doing things for others	Hours I *wanted* to do things for others	Number of times I let others help me	Number of times I asked for help	Number of things I agreed to do that I don't want to do or am not sure I want to do	Number of times I said "no" or "probably not" to requests	Number of times I offered to do less than was asked	Number of times I said I'd think about it instead of "yes"

19 Chapter | Catastrophizing? Accepting Uncertainty

Do you often worry about a tragedy happening to you or a loved one?

When someone you care about is late, do you worry that they are dead or badly injured?

Do you worry that your children will be abducted? And do you worry that they have been abducted if they are even a little late?

Do you worry the entire time someone you love is traveling or even commuting?

When you or someone you love has a headache, are you worried that it's brain cancer or an aneurism? Or something similar?

If you said "no" to all of the above questions, skip to the next chapter. If you said "yes" only to the last question, read this chapter, but Chapter 21 (on hypochondriasis) will probably be more helpful for you. If you said "yes" to any of the other questions, continue.

Life is uncertain. We are vulnerable and we are mortal. Bad things, even horrific things, happen in life. We are all fearful of catastrophic events, but most of us accept the uncertainty of life. **We realize that worrying about the unlikely possibility of these events is fruitless.** It's better to enjoy life now regardless of whether something terrible happens tomorrow, a year from now, decades from now, or never.

If you fret about the possibility of horrific events, you have two choices. One is to accept that life is uncertain. The second is to *not* accept uncertainty and continue to fret about things over which you have little or no control, such as fatal car crashes, terrorist attacks, or unexpected medical events.

When you think about these possible tragic situations, you may feel similar to how you would feel as if one of them were actually happening. At times, you may even convince yourself that it *has* happened. You feel panicky time after time, only to be relieved when a loved one arrives home safely or the emergency room physician or cardiologist gives you or a loved one a clean bill of health. But until you get the confirmation that everything is okay, you are living in an artificial reality, feeling the emotions you would feel if the feared event were really happening.

In addition to developing a bad habit of worrying, there are three possible reasons that you may worry specifically about catastrophic events. One is that something has happened to you to make you feel this vulnerability. You have already felt this horrible pain and loss and you fear having to live through another painful event. Interestingly, people who have lost a parent or been separated from a parent prior to the age 17 are much more likely to suffer from generalized anxiety disorder and depression (Kendler, Neale, Kessler, Heath, & Eaves, (1992). If this has happened to you, you may feel more vulnerable. The second is that someone close to you has suffered a tragic event. Supporting them and feeling their pain has left you feeling worried about such a tragedy happening to you. If any of these situations apply to you and this workbook doesn't lead to satisfactory results, you may want to see a therapist who specializes in trauma. Processing these events with EMDR (eye-movement desensitization and reprocessing), prolonged exposure, and other experiential strategies can be particularly helpful.

The third possibility is that repeatedly seeing tragic events in the news can sensitize you to the possibility that you, too, could be a victim. Even hearing about a tragedy through word of mouth can affect us. Hundreds of years ago, we heard only of tragedies in our own communities and in neighboring communities. In addition, terrorism wasn't as common then and weapons are becoming increasingly deadly. Finally, automobiles have exponentially increased the likelihood of tragic events, not to mention safer forms of modern-day transportation that still add to the threat of tragedy. Avoiding watching the news isn't always effective, as we may still hear about these painful events on social media and in conversation. However, it might be helpful to limit watching news coverage. It's certainly worth experimenting for a week or so to see whether you feel better.

With all of the horrible things that happen in the world, it's understandable that you want to try to control them by preventing them from happening. The fact is that worry will not prevent tragedies. The irony is that the very things you are doing to try to control your life are actually making your life more out of control. Your worry about these events may frustrate others. You may be irritable or find it difficult to concentrate, sleep, or relax. You might have headaches, have stomach aches, or feel nervous or jittery much of the time. Maybe you are fatigued from wearing yourself out with anxiety.

Describe the ways in which your worry about catastrophic events makes your life more out of control.

_____

_____

_____

Keeping this in mind, on a scale of 0–10, how much are your worries about catastrophes controlling your life in a negative way? (0 = no negative impact, 10 = completely controlling your life.)

_____

Now consider to what extent your worries are giving you control—that is, to what extent do you believe your worries are helping to prevent bad things from happening? What is your level of control over tragic events on a scale from 0–10? (0 = no control, 10 = complete control.)

_____

Hopefully, you are more motivated than ever to manage your worries about tragedy now that you are more clearly seeing that your worry about catastrophic events is controlling your life in a negative way while making it no less likely that they will happen. Worry prevents you from enjoying life fully. Furthermore, you may find yourself in your eighties without having suffered a significant tragedy and regret having spent your life worrying about things that never even happened.

However, if you rated your level of control above a 2, you likely have a false sense of control. In this case, read the next chapter—"Superstitious? What's the Evidence?"—to address this. However, you may continue to work on this chapter first.

Regardless of why you catastrophize, it can be helpful to think of your reaction as an artificial reality, alternate reality, or simply "fiction." In fact, you can simply label these types of thoughts. Remember in Chapter 4 when you practiced labeling your worries as "new" or "repeat" and as "helpful" or "not helpful"? If you found that exercise useful, labeling your worries as "fact" or "fiction" should be particularly helpful when you are catastrophizing. Label a thought as "fact" when you know it is true and "fiction" when you make up a story in your mind about the worst possible scenarios. Even in the very rare event that things do turn out poorly, it's never exactly as you imagine, so labeling these thoughts as "fiction" is accurate. It may also help you to come up with facts that are helpful. For example, if you're worried that your spouse or child has been in a car accident and you begin to label these thoughts as "fiction," perhaps one of the following facts may also come to mind: "I've worried about this hundreds of times and the worst thing that happened was a fender-bender," "Worrying about it won't give me control over it," or "If there's been an accident they're more likely to be caught in the traffic than involved in the accident." Also try labeling your thoughts as "useful" or "not useful" because these worries are never, or very rarely, useful. If they are useful, they are only useful insofar as problem-solving can be accomplished (e.g., take a different route or stop at a hotel if winter driving conditions are dangerous).

If you are like most people who suffer from this type of worry, you recognize the futility. You realize that worrying about it won't change the outcome and you probably also recognize that things usually turn out better than you feared. Even when things turn out poorly, you recognize that, had you worried more, it wouldn't have had a positive effect on the outcome. Unfortunately, even though you know these things, it hasn't changed your habit. You continue to worry. The good news is that, if thinking of these thoughts as an alternate reality or artificial reality, labeling "fact" or "fiction," or using other labels isn't helpful enough, the self-monitoring form on page 99 has been very useful for many people. It can help you to internalize reality such that you can likely begin to feel the futility of these worries in a way you haven't before.

People who worry excessively about tragedy may check things excessively or avoid situations that are generally safe. See Chapter 15 for more information about how to stop these behaviors.

The following are examples of safety behaviors that you may want to stop or reduce. Engaging in these behaviors negatively reinforces these behaviors. They are likely to raise anxiety and make you exaggerate the likelihood that a tragedy will occur.

- Checking doors and windows.
- Calling or texting to check up on a loved one who is traveling.
- Insisting that a loved one contact you at every leg of a trip.
- Excessive prayers for safety. Honor your religious practices, but avoid increasing your praying to manage your worry.
- Texting or calling a loved one who is only a few minutes late.

- Avoiding driving in any number of situations. For example, avoiding driving on highways, in the rain, at night, or in new places.
- Bringing along a "safety" person. (There is safety in numbers in some situations such that it may be healthy to bring a person along. However, try to go alone when you feel compelled to bring a person along who only makes you "feel" safe and when that person is not truly providing protection or the level of protection is greatly exaggerated.)
- Overusing alarms, mace, or weapons when in a generally safe area.

All these can be used as crutches that can negatively reinforce your fears and strengthen these fears in the long run. If you didn't already address these when reading Chapter 15, on removing crutches, consider using the monitoring form on p. 77.

If you are having difficulty letting go of these worries because you think that worrying can either prevent tragedy or reduce the emotional pain you feel if a tragedy does occur, then read the next chapter.

On the form on the next page, make an entry for everything you worry about that you are likely to know the outcome of within about a month. Just write enough that you will recognize your worry; details aren't necessary. However, feel free to write details if you believe it will be helpful for you to get them out of your mind and onto paper.

Once you have recorded a worry on the form, wait until you learn the outcome of the worry. When you know the outcome, write a brief description of what actually happened and assign a number that best describes that outcome using the key at the top of the form. Most of the time, you will do nothing more. However, if the outcome is as bad or worse than you feared, decide how well you handled it and assign the appropriate rating. Use the same ratings for the outcome and how you handled it. Then in a month or so look back at your ratings and note how many of the worries turned out better than you feared. If you are like most people, engaging in this monitoring will help you to internalize these things that your wise mind knows to be true, but that your worried mind currently still frets about. After a few weeks, it is likely you will internalize the fact that worry is futile, even harmful, and that things usually turn out better than you had feared.

Feel free to add other worries. In other words, you don't have to restrict this monitoring form to catastrophic worries. It can be helpful to record any worry you expect to learn the outcome of soon.

Worry Outcome Diary

1 = Much better than feared   2 = Better than feared   3 = About the same as feared   4 = Worse than feared   5 = Much worse than feared

Worry	Reality	Outcome Rating	If 3 or Above, How I Handled It	Am I Glad I Worried About It?

20 Chapter | Superstitious? What's the Evidence?

Are you afraid that if you stop worrying, bad things will happen?

Do you worry about bad things happening because, if they do happen, you believe it will be less painful?

If either of these beliefs fuel your worries, they are probably attempts to control things you cannot control. However, instead of giving you control over worried-about outcomes, they actually make your life more out of control. If neither of these apply to you, skip this chapter.

Only the first worry is truly superstitious. Sometimes we have a healthy concern that can help to protect people. Being concerned and engaging in planning and problem-solving isn't superstitious. Some may argue that prayer is superstitious, but those who pray believe a higher power can help them.

If you suffer from superstitious worries, you believe that worrying about a situation can have a protective effect. For instance, if your daughter is driving back to college, it doesn't hurt to check the car to see that it is operating properly and check that the tires are in good condition. It may not hurt to suggest that she pull over to the side of the road if she is tired or suggest she find someone to ride with her. A prayer for safe travels prior to her departure is reasonable. But if you believe that worrying will increase the likelihood that she will make it to her destination safely and you worry until she calls to let you know she made it, you suffer from superstitious worry. The next worksheet can help you to rethink this habit.

If you think that worrying about something bad happening will cushion the blow if and when it happens, you *may* be right. However, there are several reasons I recommend that you stop this. The way we treat this problematic habit overlaps with superstitious worry.

Hopefully, answering the questions above led you to begin to question your superstitious beliefs so as to help you to reduce your worry. The world is beautiful and there are many wonderful things about it. Unfortunately, though, bad things happen that can negatively affect our lives forever and even end our lives and the lives of loved ones. It makes sense that you would want to do everything you can to avoid getting laid off, losing a loved one to a tragedy, or making a costly mistake. Unfortunately, other than taking reasonable problem-solving measures, there is nothing you can do to prevent most of the things that you are trying to control with your superstitious worries. The irony is that, in an attempt to control fate or serendipity, you actually become more out of control with worry and anxiety. Depression or dysthymia (chronic low-level depression) can even set in from feeling that something awful could strike at any moment. To paraphrase a quote from rapper, Wiz Khalifa: "Worrying is stupid. It's like walking around with an umbrella, waiting for it to rain." And I will add that when you do this, you often block out the sun. Or, in most cases, worry is interest paid on a debt that never comes due.

Superstition

How do you think this process works? Explain to the best of your ability how you think the thoughts in your head affect your loved ones who are miles away.

_____

_____

What evidence do you have that your thoughts *do* protect your loved ones?

_____

_____

If there is anything else that you are worried about superstitiously, such as losing your job or worrying about your performance on a test or interview, how do you believe the thoughts in your head keep it from happening?

_____

_____

Is it possible that, had you not worried, or had you worried significantly less, the events in your life would have turned out very similar, except that you would be more relaxed and happier?

☐ Yes   ☐ No

Do you think that worrying gives you a false sense of control? That is, on some level, do you feel like you are doing something about your worry that gives you a sense of control over it that you like?

☐ Yes   ☐ No

In what ways do these worries cause your life to be more out of control? For example, does your worry and anxiety cause you to be irritable, to lose sleep, to lose concentration, to feel physical discomfort, or otherwise interfere with your life?

_____

_____

_____

_____

Close your eyes and imagine what your life will be like if you reject your superstitious beliefs and stop the worry associated with them. How will it be different?

_____

_____

_____

Let's think about when we attempt to use worry to reduce shock and pain. First of all, if you worry about tragedy because you think it will help you to prevent some of the pain when tragedy strikes, you are gambling. Moreover, you are betting that something awful will happen to you. Day after day, year after year, you suffer from worry. Each day you are betting on an unlikely scenario and the payoff in that unlikely event would bring you no gain, only the possibility of a somewhat lower loss. Even if you do suffer a tragedy and you feel a little less shocked and a little less pain, will it be worth it? And, because we can never predict the kind of tragedy that will occur, if it does, will your efforts really help to prepare you? If tragedy strikes, you will still experience a great deal of pain and still be unprepared to deal with it.

If you still feel a desire to worry and believe a bit of a cushion is worth the gamble, how much do you need to worry to reduce shock and pain? Chances are you're not sure how much is enough. I recommend that you begin by worrying on a daily basis for about 15 minutes. This could be on a walk or commute, during your child's nap time or tea time, or during any other time you carve out of each day. Some clients feel better if they write about their worry in a journal and then mindfully close the journal to signify going on with life until the next worry session. If you still worry in between sessions, use the postponement technique in Chapter 6. If this is enough for you to feel as though you have done due diligence, give yourself the weekend off. Experiment by gradually reducing the time: three times per week, then twice, then once, and so on. You may even be able to get down to once per month or stop. If at any point the worry becomes problematic again, increase the frequency or duration of your planned worrying sessions.

21 Chapter | Hypochondriasis

Do you worry about aches and pains?

Do you overreact to symptoms in your body such as feeling foggy, noticing your heart beating, numbness or tingly sensations, or being light headed?

Do you jump to the conclusion that those symptoms are signs of a fatal, progressive, or chronic illness such as cancer, multiple sclerosis, or ALS (amyotrophic lateral sclerosis, also known as Lou Gehrig's disease)?

Do you search the internet looking at symptoms and diseases for more than 20 minutes a day?

Do you go to the doctor, urgent care, or emergency room often and insist on the health care professionals running more tests?

Do you question whether the tests are accurate and whether the doctors are missing something?

If you answered "yes" to any of these questions, continue reading this chapter. Otherwise, skip to the next chapter.

People struggling with hypochondriasis catastrophize that even mild symptoms may mean a chronic or fatal illness, often despite having multiple tests all indicating a clean bill of health. There is a pattern of worrying about a condition or disease for several months, even years, and then sometimes eventually feeling quite certain that you don't have that problem. Unfortunately, though, it's not long before a new disease becomes the focus of worry, and sometimes worries about a disease you've worried about in the past return.

Unlike worry about tragedies such as accidents, being a victim of terrorism, or being robbed, for example, we do have some control over our health. In fact, we do sometimes hear of people who went to several doctors before a disease was correctly identified and treated. We also occasionally hear of more grim circumstances in which the issue is identified only after it's too late, even upon autopsy. So the concern about underusing medical care is a real one. The importance of catching medical issues early was even mentioned in Chapter 13. All these facts explain why reducing the worry associated with hypochondriasis is challenging and why some people worry about their health so much.

The good news is that, even when there is something seriously wrong, getting the right help requires problem-solving, which can be done with minimal anxiety. Tenacity, not anxiety, is the best approach when you have a persistent concerning symptom. Also good news is that there are strategies to help dismiss minor recurrent symptoms.

Most people with hypochondriasis overuse the medical system. That is, they go to doctors, urgent care, or the emergency room too much and may also use too much over-the-counter medication or request tests they don't really need. Conversely, some people who are overly worried about medical symptoms *avoid* seeking care because they are terrified of getting bad news. For the reasons stated two paragraphs back, it is recommended that you see a physician if you are having symptoms that could be the signs of a medical problem. Waiting too long to address symptoms that can be treated could lead to a self-fulfilling prophecy of a serious medical condition. In other words, when medical problems such as multiple sclerosis, cancer, and certain infections are caught early, they are easily treated. Wait too long and the situation could be more serious.

While some symptoms are signs of a serious problem, most aches, pains, and otherwise unpleasant symptoms are idiosyncratic, benign issues that usually pass. While anxiety doesn't cause the most feared diseases like cancer and ALS, stress does affect immune function that can contribute to some disease processes. Furthermore often anxiety and worry directly cause physical symptoms. When stressed, our sympathetic nervous system activates our bodies in a way that helps us to fight and run to keep us safe in the face of danger. But when we are stressed with no place to go and nobody to fight, it can cause gastrointestinal distress, high-blood pressure, tachycardia, headaches, and skin disorders. Realizing that their symptoms are caused by stress, most people dismiss them. For others, these natural physiological responses may lead to worry that something is seriously wrong. For instance, tachycardia and palpitations may trigger worry about a heart attack or a headache may lead to worry about brain cancer. For much more information see *It's Not All in Your Head: How Worrying about Your Health Could Be Making You Sick -and What You Can Do about It* (Asmundson & Taylor, 2005).

Unless the symptom is severe and accompanied by unexpected pain, most of us typically postpone the decision to seek professional advice when we experience a new symptom. If the symptom persists for several days or gets progressively worse, we then problem-solve instead of worrying too much. Your goal is to be able to postpone worrying about most symptoms and problem-solve with minimal anxiety.

To simplify, when we have a symptom, we have five choices:

1. Postpone the decision to seek medical care.
2. Take over-the-counter or prescription medication.
3. Get help now. That is, go to urgent care or the emergency room.
4. Schedule an appointment with your doctor or nurse practitioner.
5. Worry.

When in doubt, postpone your concern to the next day. If you are unsuccessful, try a shorter time period. Even consider setting a timer for two hours. See pgs. 25-26 in Chapter 6, on postponing worry, for a summary of what to do. Also consider creating some B^3s (see Chapter 8), such as "I've worried about this same symptom before and my doctor said it's nothing to worry about," "I've had my heart checked, and while I could get a second opinion, it is likely to only feed my worries," or "No use in worrying about something that I've decided I'm not going to seek care for at this point."

Much of the advice given in Chapter 19 (on catastrophizing) can be useful for medical concerns. Experiment by labeling your thoughts and using the "Worry Outcome Diary" (p. 99) for every instance in which you worry about a symptom.

In addition, complete the Medical History Log on the next page.

Medical History Log

Complete this medical history log. Include symptoms for which you did and did not receive a diagnosis. Use the following rating scale in column four:

1 = Much better than feared   2 = Better than feared   3 = About the same as feared   4 = Worse than feared   5 = Much worse than feared

Symptoms That Have Caused Me Worry in the Past	Diagnosis or Diagnoses I Feared Were the Cause of the Symptoms	Highest Level of Anxiety About These Symptoms (1–10)	Eventual Conclusion: Description and Rating	Current Level of Anxiety About This Symptom(s) (1–10)

Looking back at each symptom or set of symptoms you worried about in the past, and thinking about the worry and the measures you took to alleviate your concerns, how would you handle each situation differently?

_____

_____

What did you learn from this exercise?

_____

_____

In Chapter 15, you read about crutches. Perhaps you included your health checking there. If not, consider what crutches you may have that feed your fear of medical problems. The following are quite common:

- Surf the internet compulsively.

- Reassure yourself repeatedly that you are okay only to quickly go back to the worry repeatedly.

- Seek reassurance from friends, family, and colleagues.

- Seek medical attention too much.

- Check your vitals excessively.

- Check your body in other ways (e.g., looking in the mirror or repeatedly checking any part of your body).

- Checking your children in much the same way as in the above examples.

- Any behavior that isn't mentioned that temporarily decreases your anxiety only to maintain or increase it.

If you have a bad habit of searching the internet, I suggest that you do a behavioral experiment. For one week, do not search the internet, do not look at internet news, and do not go on social media. Limit your computer activity to emails that are required for work. If you subscribe to any health-related websites, unsubscribe from all of them or at least mark their emails as junk so that they go into your junk file.

Once you have done this, a general rule of thumb is to only check two or three of the most trusted sites for health information. This is to limit the amount of time spent and to limit the potential for confusion from getting conflicting information from several different sites. It is also best to stick to those sites to which physicians, psychologists, and other health care professionals contribute. There is a plethora of misinformation on the internet and sometimes it even occurs on sites that you might think could be trusted. *Always* be wary of information on the internet. The best approach to dealing with your symptoms is to make a running list of questions and concerns and bring them to your doctor. Be careful about this, too, as there is the risk of spending too much time and energy making such a list.

Two sites that I recommend are WebMD.com and MayoClinic.org, because physicians and other health care professionals are involved in the content. If you have concerns about your children, Healthychildren.org is powered by pediatricians at the American Academy of Pediatrics. Even these sites should be used sparingly. Avoid using the links on these three sites that take you to additional sites! If you are spending more than 20 minutes per day looking up information, if you feel you have the information you need but feel compelled to continue to look, or if you're feeling increasingly anxious, it's best you stop. If you are still concerned hours later, plan to call your doctor for advice. Remember there is no substitute for the years of training and experience your doctor brings you along with their knowledge of you and your medical history. Your physician can also examine you and assess your symptoms more carefully—things an internet site cannot do. To help yourself stop or reduce your searching, think about how you'd rather be spending your time and try to switch activities.

What would you rather do than search the internet?

_____   _____

_____   _____

_____   _____

_____   _____

22 Chapter | Procrastination

The jury is in! Procrastination, like much of everything else in life, is best done in moderation. Those who procrastinate too long, of course, are likely to fail. Pre-crastinators (those who get everything done well in advance) do fine, but they are not the people who are the most successful. It turns out that the people who are the most successful procrastinate in a way that is efficient and inspires creativity.

Planned procrastination is designed for those who are successful procrastinators but have worry, guilt, or both about their habit. If you believe that the benefits of your procrastination outweigh the cons, use the worksheet on the next page.

If you procrastinate and it often fails you, the Planned Procrastination Worksheet is not for you. Whether you have difficulty getting motivated for dull and boring tasks due to inertia or whether it is because you're overwhelmed and just can't get started on your long to-do list or huge project, you probably tell yourself that you should do it. But you really don't want to do it. Thinking about why you do want to complete a task can be helpful. Therefore, the Find the Want worksheet on p. 40 is useful.

Moreover, the key to overcoming problematic procrastination is to commit to small, easily accomplished pieces. It's helpful to remember the adage "inch by inch it's a cinch; yard by yard it's hard." You can apply this premise in two general ways. The first is to divide big projects into subtasks. The second way is to commit to a reasonable, specific amount of time to work on your project each day, a few times a week, or even once a week.

An example that many of you can relate to is a messy house. If every room in your house is a mess, it is likely to feel overwhelming to think of cleaning it. You look around and lose any motivation you may have had because it is so overwhelming and it seems that any efforts would barely make a dent. The result: You give up.

In this case, it helps to start by picking one room that you feel would provide the greatest stress relief if it could be clean. Let's say it's the kitchen. That still might feel like an overwhelming task, but not nearly as daunting as cleaning your whole place. The next step is to pick one kitchen task that would be easy to accomplish, preferably something that would take less than 15 minutes. For instance, you could commit to throwing away all the trash. Or you may decide to put away everything on the countertops and tables. If you have a fair amount of motivation, you may decide to do both.

At this point, one of two things will happen. One possibility is that you will feel unmotivated to do anything else. If this is the case, at least celebrate your small but important feat. You finally got started! Make a commitment to do the next task the next day, or, if today is a weekend or day off, you might even commit to doing it later in the day.

Planned Procrastination
for Successful Procrastinators

What are you currently procrastinating about?

_____

Based on your history, when do you think you will start this task? Be realistic.

_____

Take out your calendar and write down the date and time you think you will likely start this project. If in doubt, choose the earliest you would realistically start based on past behavior.

If you worry in between, remind yourself that procrastination always works for you and postpone your worry to the date you have put in your calendar. Alternatively, begin the "Inch by Inch" worksheet later in this chapter.

Feeling guilty? Make a list of people to whom you would like to explain why you are going to continue to procrastinate.

_____   _____

_____   _____

Ask for their support. Preferably discuss this in person. Here is an example of a script.

> I know my procrastination makes you uncomfortable, but procrastination has always worked very well for me. I've done well in school and in my jobs. When I start things early, I spend more time dawdling and distracted. Once I start working, I'm very efficient and more creative. The worst thing is that I occasionally don't get enough sleep. But that's worth it to me. I know you do things differently, but the way that I do things really works for me. I've even read recently that moderate procrastinators are actually the most successful people. So I'm hoping I can get your support and that you can view my procrastination as being different, instead of viewing it as wrong.

If you cannot talk to the person (e.g., if they are deceased, but you still "hear their voice" in your head) or there is a reason you don't want to talk to them, you can write them a letter you don't send or pretend they are sitting in an empty chair and say something similar. You could write an email, but remember that email exchanges on sensitive topics risk being misunderstood. If the person is not accepting and continues to judge you, consider letting them be responsible for their anxiety or frustration. You can also use the broken-record strategy to let them know you are firm in your habits. For example, any time they judge you, repeatedly reply, "Procrastination works for me." Soon they will likely tire of your response and stop.

The other thing that might happen is that by accomplishing this task you feel energized. You might think, "It would be pretty easy to clean off the countertops and they'll look so much better." In just a few minutes, you have clean countertops. You might stop at this point and be proud of your accomplishment. Then again, you might think, "I may as well load the dishes in the sink into the dishwasher" or "I may as well do the dishes." If you get this far, the only thing left would be the floor, and that would be an easy task for the next day. Or, if you have time and energy, you might just find yourself finishing the job.

An alternative to choosing a small task is to spend a certain amount of time a project. Depending on your motivation level and the type of task, you might commit to only 10 minutes, or you might commit to a couple of hours. Much like the subtasks, you might spend 15 minutes cleaning your kitchen, for example, and then decide that you are on a roll and want to continue. At this point, you could set a goal for an additional 10–15 minutes or you could just continue at will. Setting a timer may help you to focus your attention on the tasks at hand. Do your best not to be distracted by your phone, by reading junk mail, or by other things that would take your attention off the task. Be fast and focused, but not rushed. Think of it as a game to see how much you can accomplish while being mindful and keeping your body relatively relaxed.

Whether you choose small tasks or small chunks of time may vary depending upon the task. The chunk of time will certainly vary depending upon the task. For example, choosing 15 minutes when you're painting a room or mowing a lawn doesn't make sense. If you like the work, a larger time period will be more effective than if the task is something you really don't want to do.

A third option is to combine the above strategies. Set a small goal and give yourself a time limit to accomplish that goal. Think of it as a deadline. Consider how much you would typically be able to accomplish in those final moments, after you stop procrastinating and finally get started. For instance, say you are writing a term paper. Commit to writing a draft that is at least three double-spaced pages in an hour. Write down the time that you plan to finish this task and don't do anything that you'd avoid doing if you were down to the final deadline. The idea is to mimic the focus you get after you finally get started when a real deadline is looming. When you've finished, reward yourself, even if it is just taking a 10–15 minute break. In the following worksheet, try to choose a task that you have plenty of time to finish. Or, if you have already been procrastinating, it's okay to use it now, but when you finish it remember to use it to prevent yourself from procrastinating in the future.

Another strategy to combat procrastination is preparation. If you have been avoiding a task, set out the necessary equipment and any required clothing ahead of time. For instance, in the case of the aforementioned kitchen, let's say that you had done almost everything, but had run out of time or energy to do the floor. It would take you about a minute to get out the broom, dustpan, bucket, mop, and soap. Then, the next day, it will be easier to keep on task.

Time yourself on tasks you tend to avoid because you don't like them. You will probably realize that you overreact to the gravity of the task. For instance, most people are surprised by how little time it takes to unload the dishwasher or put away a basket of folded laundry if they're focused. Timing tasks can help to prevent dawdling as well. In fact, you can look at this as a game. I'm going to try to put away the clothes in less than five minutes…go!

Is there a small task that you have been avoiding? Has it been hanging over your head for days, weeks, even months? Maybe it's a phone call to schedule an appointment? Maybe you're avoiding putting the clothes away from your laundry basket or changing the furnace filter you bought two weeks ago. If you have a few minutes, don't delay! Do it right now. Or, if it's something you can't do now, write in your planner to do it later today or tomorrow. If you have several little things like this hanging over your head, do one a day until they are all finished. Because life is full of these small tasks that we tend to postpone, some people find it helpful to set a regular time in their schedule to do just one of them. For instance, you might choose to do one small task before you eat lunch or just after you finish or return from lunch.

Inch by Inch

What is the most important task you want to avoid procrastinating about?

_____

_____

Which strategy do you like most for this task: dividing it into small tasks, choosing a chunk of time, or both?

_____

_____

When do you want to complete the larger task?

_____

_____

How many days do you have to complete this task?

_____

_____

Look at your calendar and see what other commitments you have. Schedule an amount of time for each day or many of the remaining days, or divide the task into subtasks and enter time amounts or subtasks into your calendar.

THIS IS A CINCH

23 | Perfectionism

Chapter

If you are only perfectionistic in one or two areas of your life, you may not think of yourself as perfectionistic. Having a desire to be a great parent, having a solid work ethic, or having the desire to be the best athlete or musician you can be are all healthy, within reason. But standards that are too high, even in one area of life, can cause anxiety, frustration, disappointment, and a lack of balance that often leads to depression. It can also strain relationships when you judge others who do not embrace your excessively high standards. Areas in which people commonly have unrealistic standards include work in general, neatness, organization, writing, personal appearance, and diet and exercise. **If you believe your very high standards in any area of your life are causing anxiety, anger, frustration, or depression, this chapter can be helpful.**

One mistake that many people make is that all of their priorities are school or work. Do you sometimes think that you'll read a book, go shopping, see a movie, go out with your friends, or have a night with just your spouse as soon as you catch up on your work? Only, that rarely happens? Do you feel guilty, anxious, or both when you aren't productive, so you rarely stop to enjoy living? Even when you do engage in social events that aren't productive, are they usually work, charitable, or family obligations?

When you rarely do things that are fun and relaxing, depression or dysthymia are inevitable. The best way to overcome this is to think about the things you would love to do, that you used to like to do, or that you don't do nearly as much as you'd like to do. Carve out some time weekly to do these things regardless of what comes up.

When part of why you engage in perfectionistic behaviors is to avoid feeling anxious, guilty, or self-conscious, you are strengthening your habit with negative reinforcement. The more you do this, the more guilty and anxious you feel when you consider taking time for leisurely activities or otherwise loosening your standards. If you want to find more balance in your life, it is necessary for you to engage in activities such as socializing, reading, or watching TV, and let yourself feel uncomfortable. The more you do this, the less anxious and guilty you will feel and the more you will begin to enjoy these activities. If you are so accustomed to working excessively that you don't even know what you like, explore lists of hobbies online to see whether something appeals to you and think about what you liked to do before adult obligations presented themselves.

Evaluating and Changing
Your Perfectionism

How does your perfectionism make your life less perfect?

_____

_____

What are the advantages of your perfectionism?

_____

_____

Are there areas of perfectionism you think are working well for you?

_____

_____

In what area, or areas, of your life is your perfectionism causing problems?

_____

_____

What are the disadvantages of your perfectionism in these areas?

_____

_____

_____

What are the things you'd have more time to do if you lived a more balanced life?

_____

_____

Describe how a balanced life would affect your depression and anxiety.

_____

_____

Is perfectionism causing problems with your mental health? Are you unhappy? Stressed? Losing sleep? Irritable? Do you have difficulty concentrating? Elaborate.

_____

_____

_____

How is it affecting your health?

_____

_____

How often do you abuse substances to deal with your stress around perfectionism?

_____

_____

How is it affecting your relationships at home and work?

_____

_____

Do you find yourself getting angry or irritated with people who don't meet your standards? If yes, write how it is affecting them and, consequently, you.

_____

_____

Do you spend 50% more time, for example, making something only about 5% better? Describe.

_____

_____

If so, do you think that 5% makes a difference a week later?

_____

What would your life be like if you lowered your standards by 20%? 30%? More? Close your eyes and visualize what this would be like and write your answer here.

_____

_____

What are you afraid you would lose if you lowered your standards?

_____

_____

How likely is it that your fears will occur?

_____

How likely is it that the benefits of lowering your standards will outweigh the risks?

_____

If you do want to lower your standards, how far do you want to go? 20%? 30%? 50%?

_____

How will you do it? Write a plan to reduce your standards by the percentage you chose as your answer to the previous question.

_____

_____

_____

How do you think you acquired these high standards? (Usually they are learned from one or both parents, a competitive school, teachers, or coaches, but sometimes siblings and friends can play a role.)

_____

_____

_____

What would you say to the person (or people) you named in your previous answer now if you could do so without consequences? Consider writing a letter you don't send, telling them in person, or pretending they are in an empty chair and telling them how you feel.

_____

_____

_____

_____

Consider creating a successful life rather than aiming to be a success. Pam Houston (2000) put it beautifully as she redefined success in her memoir:

> *My first notion of success, came from my parents and involved country clubs, clothing, and cars. As I became an adult I replaced that list with a list of my own, no less arbitrary: a Ph.D., a book of short stories, a place on a best-seller list, a film. But now I am coming to the understanding that success has less to do with the accumulation of things and more to do with an accumulation of moments, and that creating a successful life might be as simple as determining which moments are the most valuable, and seeing how many of those I can string together in a line.*

Consider the case of Bob Jones and Bob Smith. Jones is the CEO of a medium-sized company. He makes a seven-figure income and lives in a mansion with his wife and two kids, but he doesn't get to spend much time with them because he works a minimum of 70 hours a week. His job is a means to an income; he doesn't usually enjoy it. He loves to play golf but rarely gets to play, and when he does, it's usually with business associates.

Smith is in sanitation. Essentially, he's a garbage collector who makes a meager income and lives in a small three-bedroom apartment with his wife and two kids. He only works 40 hours a week, so he gets a lot of quality time with them. He loves his job because it's active, he likes being outdoors, and the guys he works with are a lot of fun. He loves to bowl and gets to do so at least once a week with friends.

Certainly, by traditional standards, Bob Jones is much more successful. But who enjoys life more? Whose life would you rather lead? Who will have the fewest regrets on his death bed? Whose *life* is more successful?

AFRAID OF LOSING YOUR EDGE?

If you feel you can't relax because you are afraid you will lose your edge, you may believe that the higher your stress, the higher your productivity. This is a myth. The Yerkes–Dodson law (Yerkes & Dodson, 1908) proved that the relationship between arousal (often experienced as stress and anxiety) and productivity yields a bell-shaped curve such that a moderate level of arousal yields the greatest level of performance or productivity. In other words, increasing your arousal level (energy/alertness) improves your performance up to a point. After this moderate point, higher levels of arousal result in declining performance (see Figure below). The Yerkes–Dodson law proved that, regardless of what the activity is, if someone is too relaxed or unmotivated, performance will suffer. However, performance suffers every bit as much when someone is overly stressed. Think about when you are really stressed. Your thoughts are racing or jumbled, and you may find it difficult to concentrate. You may make mistakes, become forgetful, or spend too much time attempting to make something perfect with little return. You could freeze and draw a blank in conversation or thought. You might become irritable and difficult to be around such that working with others becomes counterproductive. People may be less likely to help and support you.

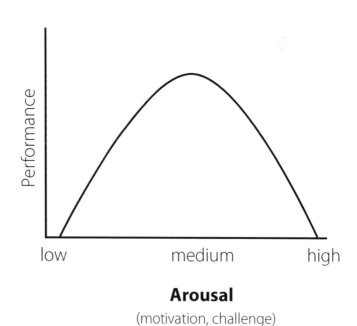

Arousal
(motivation, challenge)

If your perfectionism and work drive cause anxiety, you will find that by systematically reducing it, you will enjoy a corresponding increase in productivity, rather than the decrease you may fear. Perhaps you have already experienced this by following the premises in this workbook. If you've been afraid to use them, maybe you will begin to experiment with them to see whether they help your productivity or, at least, don't reduce it.

It is helpful to think about how you feel when you are "on a roll." When you are most productive and efficient, you are at a moderate level of arousal. You are alert, motivated, and focused, but not stressed and anxious. If you consider only the aspect of productivity, your goal is to be moderately motivated and challenged rather than highly stressed and anxious. However, because most of us work several hours per day, it's helpful to be to the left of that curve to conserve energy. Being in the moment and keeping your muscles relatively relaxed will help you to be at the optimal level for productivity. In fact, when you *are* most productive, you are likely in the moment and not very tense.

Hopefully, you are now motivated to reduce your perfectionistic standards. Begin to make leisure time a priority. By resisting the urge to take extra time to perfect things in favor of being good enough and by living at a moderate level of arousal, you will save time for more balance to help you lead a successful *life*.

Improve Balance

To help keep you on track, complete the following self-monitoring form daily. The goal is to increase awareness to improve balance, so do not worry about being accurate, estimates are preferable. The last column is an optional space to write in a personal goal.

Date	Hours Spent Working at My Job	Hours Spent Doing Chores and Errands	Hours Spent on Leisure Activities*	# Times I "Gave In" to My Perfectionism	# Times I Resisted the Urge to Engage in My Perfectionism**	Personal Goal

* If gardening is a hobby you truly enjoy, place the time under leisure activities. If you are in doubt about whether you should record, say, yard-work or decorating the house under work or leisure, count it as half and half. For example, if you spend two hours doing yard-work and you would rather be doing yard-work than other chores and enjoy it, but not as much as reading a book, place one hour under leisure activities and one hour under chores and errands.

** Give yourself credit for compromises, even if small.

24 | Closing Comments
Chapter

Hopefully, this workbook has been helpful. If it wasn't very helpful, was it because you only read through it and didn't engage in many of the exercises, worksheets, and self-monitoring tasks? If so, consider going back to the beginning and doing all or most of them. If you did apply most of the activities and were unsuccessful, consider the following:

1. If you don't have a therapist, consider finding one by asking your doctor or friends. Rather than picking one at random, try the Anxiety and Depression Association of America website (Adaa.org), choose "Find Help," then choose "Find a Therapist."

2. Consider seeing your doctor to rule out the various physiological reasons why you might be depressed or anxious. See p. 179-180 of the Therapists' Guide for more information.

3. Consider getting medication for your depression or anxiety. I recommend avoiding benzodiazepines (see p. 157 in the Therapists' Guide for additional information). I also recommend that you see a psychiatrist rather than another physician.

4. If you really don't want to see a therapist, it may be helpful to read the corresponding chapters of the Therapists' Guide while going back through the workbook.

**For your convenience, purchasers can download and
print worksheets and handouts from www.pesi.com/worry**

Part 2 | Therapists' Guide

Worry:
The Root of Anxiety and Depression

Generalized anxiety disorder (GAD) is one of the most common co-morbid disorders among anxiety and depressive disorders. In other words, if a client has more than one anxiety disorder or has an anxiety disorder and a depressive disorder, the likelihood that one of those disorders is GAD is high. Eighty-two percent of clients with a principal diagnosis of GAD have at least one co-morbid diagnosis (Brown & Barlow, 1992). Furthermore, GAD usually presents prior to the other disorders. Therefore, excessive worry appears to be a breeding ground, putting individuals at risk for other anxiety disorders and depression. In addition, GAD is associated with a variety of medical disorders including, but not limited to, headaches, cardiovascular disease, and skin disorders (Newman, 2000). Gastrointestinal distress is a particularly problematic symptom of anxiety. In a study conducted at Penn State University, we found that 72.5% of individuals with GAD reported gastrointestinal symptoms, most reporting moderate to severe symptoms. This was compared to only 19.5% in the control group, with none reporting severe symptoms and most reporting mild symptoms (Abel & Borkovec, 1995). Moreover, Lee and his colleagues (2009) found that individuals with GAD are 4.7 times more likely to have irritable bowel syndrome. Similarly, patients with irritable bowel syndrome are five times more likely to have GAD.

People often get accustomed to excessive worry and they often don't realize the degree to which their habit has led to depression, medical problems, and more serious anxiety and compulsive disorders such as obsessive–compulsive disorder (OCD) and panic disorder. Clients may present to therapy with depression or panic, for instance, and may not even mention that they worry excessively. Their panic or depression is of much greater concern and they often don't consider the possibility that their worry habit can change. Therefore, it is important to ask every client you see how much they worry and assess for, and treat, GAD. This is true even when the client doesn't complain of anxiety.

While this book is not designed to directly treat phobias, OCD, social anxiety, or panic disorder, when individuals with GAD have one or more co-morbid conditions and are treated for GAD, the co-morbid conditions improve significantly (Borkovec, Abel, & Newman, 1995). Also, when individuals work their way into a panicked state, treating the worry that begins that spiral is usually very helpful.

Consider waiting to give your client the workbook until after you have used the exercises through Chapter 4. In short, these experiential exercises often work best when not preceded by an explanation. Engaging in the workbook can then reinforce what you've done in the first few chapters. Starting with Chapter 5 it is okay if the client works with you or even ahead of you. However, encourage them to read and apply no more than one chapter per week from Chapter 5 forward.

Fighting Worry and Anxiety Fuels It

Read what Chapter 2 says about the "white bear research" conducted by Wegner (1989). Demonstrate this phenomenon to your client, preferably before they read the chapter. Instead of a white bear, hold up an object or a photo for your client and tell them not to think about it. Then proceed to talk about the findings of the white bear research. You can also add Hayes and Smith's (2005) concept from their book *Get Out of Your Mind and Into Your Life*. They state that if you don't want anxiety, you will, and then go on to say that if you're willing to have anxiety, you won't. They add that if the only reason you're willing to have anxiety is to *not* have anxiety, then you're not really willing to have anxiety, and then it doesn't work. Discuss with your client that it's normal to try to fight anything that is unpleasant but that, in the case of worry and anxiety, the reality is that it makes unpleasant things worse instead of better. Encourage them to realize that between their efforts, your help, and the use of the workbook, they can learn more effective ways to manage anxiety, worry, and depression.

This fact that fighting anxiety fuels it is why we as therapists have several tools that circumvent this natural tendency to fight anxiety. When guiding relaxation, it is important that you move clients toward relaxation rather than engaging them in fighting their anxiety. For instance, in the past you may have said something like this: "Clear your mind, relax, focus on the surfaces beneath you, breathe." Instead, move toward relaxation by saying something like this: "Gently shifting your attention to the surfaces beneath you, feeling your breathing, noticing the pauses between each breath."

Other strategies that circumvent fighting anxiety include mindful acceptance, using process words instead of commands, and postponing worry. Problem-solving and cognitive therapy may be used without fighting anxiety. These strategies are very useful and recommended, but when using them, it's helpful to remember to avoid resisting anxiety.

Speaking in a Way That Is Conducive to Relaxation

You may inadvertently find yourself encouraging clients to fight anxiety, thereby fueling it. One of the most important things to remember both in sessions and when guiding relaxation is to avoid commands such as "relax" and "let it go" with clients. These command words can cause distress. Use process words such as "relaxing" or "letting go" when possible. Be mindful of when your clients are using commands in the session and gently help them to rephrase with process words, or states of being such as "relaxed" or "peaceful." In addition, be mindful of when clients are using commands when talking about applying strategies between sessions. For example, if the client says, "I was so overwhelmed yesterday and I tried to relax, but it didn't work." You might say something like:

It's so natural for us to want to fight discomfort and I know you really want to be able to relax. It's helpful, though, to remember that fighting anxiety fuels it. So, rather than trying to relax, think of the word "relaxing" while also accepting the discomfort you're feeling, allowing it to be there, and then gently moving your mind toward the present, focusing on the surfaces beneath you, and listening to the sounds you hear. Instead of trying harder, the goal is to find a balance between effort and ease.

Then you might add a metaphor for acceptance, as seen in the next chapter.

Avoid using imperatives such as "you need to" or "you should." This may place undue stress on the client. Instead, try "it would be helpful if…" or "have you considered that… ?" Another option is to suggest a behavioral experiment (for an example, see Chapter 21, p. 108): "Would you be willing to do an experiment and see what happens?" Reserve the more directive words and phrases for situations in which the client is putting themselves in danger or, possibly, for when more gentle approaches haven't motivated the client. We are more motivated to do things we *want* to do than we are to do things we think we *should* do.

It's useful for you to think of yourself as a model for your clients. If you look or sound tense, not only may it prevent your client from being able to relax, but it may also interfere with the client's ability to trust that you know what to do. It would be like an obese or visibly anorexic therapist trying to treat people with eating disorders. If you model relaxation, your client will be likely to trust that you know what you are doing. Speak at a moderate to slow pace and avoid talking too loudly, unless your client has hearing loss. See that your muscles are relaxed and that your body position shows this. Let your body and head be supported by the couch or chair behind you if you can. If you have issues with tension and anxiety, consider working your way through the workbook for yourself.

When teaching relaxation, your *patter* (the words you use when leading relaxation with clients) should have a rather slow cadence. Speaking from your diaphragm with a deep, warm voice is best. Avoid a monotone voice; allow your voice to go up and down. Use pauses in between phrases. Listen to my free recordings that go along with the client workbook at AnxietyStLouisPsychologist.com/free. For more examples, purchase the optional recordings also found on that page.

Mindful Observation and Acceptance

What is the opposite of fighting anxiety? Acceptance! When a client is able to accept anxiety, it will be alleviated. Acceptance is predominantly a right-brained, experiential phenomenon. Unfortunately, when clients read about it or when we explain it to them, there is a significant risk that they will use the left side of their brains, intellectualize, and remain stuck fighting it instead of tapping into the more experiential right side of the brain. All too often, they think that they don't want to accept it and even get threatened by the idea of accepting it. For this reason, it is best if you can use this strategy before the client reads the accompanying chapter in the workbook. Then use the chapter and worksheets to reinforce it.

I encourage you to conduct an assessment of whether the client is more troubled by their worrisome thoughts or by their physical sensations of anxiety. Sometimes this is clear. If not, you can ask:

> *If I could wave a magic wand and give you complete relief from your thoughts, but the physical sensations [here it may be helpful to name those the client experiences, such as muscle tension, nausea, or a heavy chest] would remain, or if I could wave a magic wand and the physical sensations would go away, but your thoughts would remain, which would you choose?*

If the client says "thoughts," then begin with mindful observation of the client's thoughts. (You will learn what to do later in this chapter if clients say "physical sensations.") If in doubt, begin with the thoughts because unless the client has hypochondriasis or panic attacks, the thoughts are more likely to be causing the symptoms, rather than the other way around.

When beginning with thoughts, I recommend saying to the client, "I'd like to do a little experiment and then lead you into relaxation." Then ask if they'd be willing to close their eyes. This approach is also an advantage when working with resistant clients, who are more likely to engage in "an experiment" rather than "try something" they think won't work. Here is a sample script:

> *I'd like for you to close your eyes and purposefully begin to think about something that you have been worried about that you have wanted to stop thinking about. [You might ask the client to worry specifically about something discussed earlier in the session.] [pause] Observing the thoughts that are going on in your mind [pause]. From here on out, avoiding trying to think and avoiding trying to not think. Instead, being a passive observer by just noticing the thoughts that are going on in your mind, without judgment [pause]. You may be inclined to try to think or you may be inclined to try to put the thoughts out of your mind [pause]. Doing neither [pause]. Letting go of all effort except observing any thoughts that go through your mind [pause]. Observing these thoughts almost as if you're an outsider looking in, almost as if you're watching cars drive down the street or birds flying [pause for 20–30 seconds]. Continuing to just observe the thoughts [pause for an additional 20–30 seconds].*

Some anxious clients respond very well to only observing their thoughts and will experience a reduction or cessation of their worries. These clients often automatically begin to focus on their senses and some will experience pleasant images or see colors. Others will not have quite such a positive reaction but will still have more positive or more adaptive thoughts than they had been experiencing previously. Some clients initially get frustrated, saying, "I can't think of anything." When this happens, you can respond with something like this: "Wonderful! You said you wanted to think less and your mind went blank. That's great!"

Clients are less likely to be threatened by simply observing their anxiety than by asking them to try to accept it. If you start with "Accept the feelings of anxiety in your body," clients are more likely to resist, thinking something like, "I don't want to accept it—I want to get rid of it." This will often backfire and fuel anxiety. Unfortunately, just observing may cause this reaction too, but it is less likely.

When observation alone doesn't work, adding the labeling of thoughts often does. First I simply ask that they label each thought as either a "new" or a "repeat" thought (Abel, 2010). Of course, most "repeat" thoughts are worries. And almost every worry is a repeat thought except for the very first time it is thought. I recommend following thought labeling immediately after thought observation while the client's eyes are still closed. Use the free recording "Labeling Thoughts" or follow this script for thought labeling:

> *Every thought we have is either going to be a new thought (one we haven't had before) or a repeat thought (those we have had). Given that you worry a lot, most of your thoughts are probably going to be repeat thoughts. Soon I'm going to ask you to label each thought that comes into your mind as being either "new" or "repeat": "repeat" if you've had the thought before, "new" if it's a new idea or fresh perspective. If you're not certain, don't get stuck on deciding; rather label it as "new." Continuing to just observe your thoughts. Avoiding trying to think and avoiding trying to not think, but after each thought that comes into your mind, labeling the thought aloud as either "new" or "repeat" starting now.*

Often after labeling thoughts, repeat several times, sometimes after just once, or twice, worriers begin to experience their thoughts in a new way. They not only know in their mind that repetitive worries are useless, but they also finally feel the futility of their worry in a way they haven't before this exercise. The result is often that the worries are decreased and stop involuntarily, such that the client's mind goes blank. As noted in the workbook portion, sometimes other labels work better. I begin with "new" and "repeat" because they are simple and less likely to lead to self-critical clients judging themselves for thinking "useless" thoughts.

For clients whose physical sensations bother them more than their thoughts, the free recording "Observing Emotion" or a script like the following can be useful.

> *Observing where you feel the discomfort in your body. Noticing how it feels. Observing how much space it takes up. Letting go of any judgments about how it feels. Resisting trying to push it away. Noticing where it is located. Noticing the texture of how it feels. Observing the color it feels like it would be if you could see it. Letting go of any efforts to try to change it, but if it changes, allowing it to change. If it increases, allowing it to increase, and if it decreases, allowing it to decrease. Accepting it even though it's uncomfortable. Letting go of any effort to push it away and even allowing it to stay. Just observing how you feel as if you're an outsider looking in.*

Note that the script starts with observing and moves into accepting. As noted earlier, accepting may be met with more resistance than observing.

To be clear, acceptance doesn't mean that we don't want to make an effort to let go of anxiety. Rather, we are not fighting anxiety and are gently moving toward relaxation and more helpful thoughts. Often a combination of observation, acceptance, and relaxation or cognitive therapy works best.

While this is not a book about treating panic attacks, phobias, or OCD, the same acceptance *patter* that works with worry can have a similar effect on other presentations of anxiety, as well as frustration and anger. Acceptance of the physical sensations of panic attacks can be very effective and certainly more effective than relaxation and cognitive therapy in some cases.

There are three types of clients: (1) those who can accept readily, (2) those who will never be able to accept, because they continue to feel threatened by the idea such that they keep fighting the anxiety, and (3) those who eventually connect to acceptance when the right metaphor "clicks." The workbook portion of Chapter 3 includes three of the most popular metaphors. If your client doesn't connect with the more popular metaphors, below are additional metaphors that may resonate better. Perhaps you have some of your own, too.

CHARLEY HORSE

There are many situations that cause physical discomfort in our bodies that don't cause us anxiety. One of these examples is a painful cramp in the calf, called a Charley horse. Another one is discomfort caused by stilettos or other pretty shoes that hurt one's feet. While overeating does cause anxiety for some, for those who suffer from gastrointestinal distress and don't get anxious from eating too much, this is a great analogy. Alternatively, you might find a physical discomfort that fits your client better. Begin with the Socratic method: "Does your anxiety *hurt* more or less than a Charley horse (or other physical metaphor)?" Almost all clients will respond "less." Then ask whether a Charley horse causes anxiety. Again, most clients will say "no." Then say: "Observing your anxiety as if it were a Charley horse. Allowing it to continue to feel uncomfortable, accepting it even though you don't like it." Or, if the client isn't anxious, "The next time you feel anxiety, accepting the discomfort much in the way that you do a Charley horse, which hurts but doesn't cause anxiety."

RIP CURRENT OR UNDERTOW

This is often the best metaphor for those who live near the ocean. A rip current, better known as an undertow in some areas, can push swimmers out to sea. Of course, they will be inclined to fight the current and swim against it toward the shore. However, the current will usually be too strong and efforts to swim against it will be futile, keeping one stuck in the current. Instead, swim parallel to the shore and, as the ocean permits, begin to swim at a diagonal toward the shore. Because this metaphor combines "not fighting it" with additional strategies, this may put clients who are familiar with rip currents at ease. Relinquishing control can be threatening. For some individuals, the metaphor of combining acceptance with effort to change their habits with cognitive therapy and relaxation is less threatening, and thereby more helpful.

CHINESE FINGER TRAP

The harder you try to free your fingers by pulling, the tighter the trap grips them, causing increased discomfort and moving you further from a solution. When you stop the struggle or even move in the opposite direction, the discomfort is lifted and freeing yourself with your thumbs is easy. This metaphor has data to support its efficacy! In one study, showing how the finger trap works resulted in greater reductions in anxious thoughts, physical symptoms of anxiety, and anxious avoidance than teaching breathing retraining (Eifert & Heffner, 2003).

PROCESS WORDS VS. COMMAND WORDS

The importance of using process words is discussed in Chapter 4 and Therapist Chapter 3. If your client hasn't read Chapter 4 or doesn't have the workbook, I recommend that you ask your client to close their eyes and proceed with the following experiential exercise in advance. You may do this before or after relaxation:

> *Noticing in your body where you feel anxiety or stress. Noticing how you feel when I say these three words: relax, relaxing, relaxed (pause between each word). Then repeat in reverse order: relaxed, relaxing, relax. Which one felt the best?*

Typically, clients will choose "relaxing" or "relaxed." If the client picked "relaxing," choose three additional process words (e.g., "loosening," "softening," "releasing"). You can use the words in the workbook or come up with some of your own. Repeat the above exercise, but instead of saying "relax, relaxing, relaxed" use those three new words. Note which one of the three they choose. Then do three more. Then repeat the exercise for a final time. Use the two chosen words from the additional sets of three and add "relaxing" (e.g., "loosening," "chillin'," "relaxing") to arrive at the best process word for the client.

If they chose "relaxed" instead of "relaxing," do a similar exercise using pleasant states of being, such as "peaceful," "soft," and "loose." Follow the same process to arrive at the client's best "state."

Regardless of whether you arrive at a process word (e.g., "softening") or a state (e.g., "soft"), once the client opens their eyes, ask them, "Has anyone ever told you to 'relax' or 'chill out' and you want to flip 'em off? Yet that's what we hear from others and it's often what we tell ourselves. This is why almost everyone chooses 'relaxing' or 'relaxed.'"

Encourage them to use their chosen word in lieu of the command words that they had been using when attempting to manage their anxiety. Note, however, that if they aren't relaxed, a process word might be more effective than choosing a state of being. Therefore, if they chose a state, encourage them to experiment with process words vs. states. Perhaps the process words will be more helpful when they are not relaxed and the states will help them to achieve a deeper state of relaxation if they are already relaxed.

Occasionally, clients will choose "relax" instead of "relaxing" or "relaxed." In this case, try the exercise again with "calm down," "calming," and "calm." They are much less likely to choose "calm down" than "relax" and the healthier alternatives. Then proceed as outlined above.

Don't Worry, Problem-Solve

We have long known that people with GAD tend not to problem-solve well. The question was whether (1) people with GAD are bad at problem-solving and worry as an attempt to problem-solve or (2) the anxiety present in GAD interferes with problem-solving. Dugas and his colleagues (Dugas, Letarte, Rhéaume, Freeston, & Ladouceurr, 1995), found that people with GAD were just as skilled at problem-solving than those in a control group, but it appeared that their worry and anxiety prevented them from using their skills as well.

Help clients to understand that not only is worry completely useless, but it also goes a step further. It interferes with problem-solving that might help to alleviate the concern. Therefore, the fact is that worrying about something is more likely to lead to a negative outcome. In contrast to worrying, problem-solving with little or no anxiety is much more likely to bring about an outcome that is desired.

Worries about catastrophic events (often the welfare of friends and family) and some other worries aren't amenable to problem-solving. However, helping clients to see that worry will not have a positive impact on these concerns is sometimes helpful. In conclusion, if we have no control over a concern, it is fruitless to worry about it, and when we do have some control, problem-solving is the healthiest approach.

When you see that a client has some control over something they are worried about, it can be useful for you and your client to independently brainstorm possible solutions in the session and then bring your lists together. For more detail on this process, see Chapter 5. When a client has no control over the outcome of a worry and recognizes this is useless, Chapter 6 can be very helpful. If the client believes that their worry is useful, it's usually because they have superstitious beliefs or they believe that if something tragic happens, their worry will buffer their pain. For these issues, see Chapter 20. Chapter 19 may also be helpful.

Postpone Worry

As we learned from the white bear research (see Chapter 2 and Therapist Chapter 2), trying to not worry leads to more worry. However, it turns out that we are very good at being able to postpone worry to a more convenient time. There is a clear advantage for clients to designate specific times to address their concerns. This allows them to give their concerns "due diligence" while helping to limit the amount of time they spend thinking about those concerns. Encourage clients to aim for problem-solving rather than just worry. The result is usually that they are able to control both how and when they worry, rather than their worry controlling them.

Keep in mind that some worries aren't amenable to problem-solving. For these worries, cognitive therapy or labeling the worries as "not useful" may be more helpful. Nonetheless, sometimes postponing worry to a designated time is more useful for people who feel compelled to worry even when they know there is nothing they can do about their concern. This is often the case when people worry about loved ones, particularly their children. In these instances, rule out the possibility that the person has superstitious beliefs about worry. See Therapist Chapter 20.

When the client or a family member or close friend of the client is very ill, going through a divorce, or having an otherwise unusually difficult time, some anxiety, worry, and low feelings are expected. Likewise, we expect people to grieve the loss of a family member, friend, or pet. In these instances, it's usually best for clients to express their emotions and talk about their loss with you and others, and to use journaling or other forms of emotional expression (e.g., art therapy or the two-chair technique). Nonetheless, even when emotional concerns are expected, some clients worry to an unhealthy, excessive degree. If you see that the worry is excessive and interfering with the client's functioning (e.g., causing insomnia, inability to concentrate, or anhedonia), it's good to encourage your client to have specific periods in which they talk, write, and emote. Then, when they feel they have done enough emoting for the moment, clients can postpone these worries to when they are with the loved one, to the next designated time, or to when healthy emotions are next triggered. In short, it's best for clients to fully grieve, worry, or otherwise emote, and then use coping strategies to postpone their concerns to the next appropriate time. See also Therapist Chapter 11, on accepting healthy emotion.

There are two general formats presented in the workbook to help clients postpone worries. The first worksheet (p. 25) should be used most often with most clients. This is best when clients worry about something regularly, such as work, school, children, money, health, the future, or death. Encourage your client to use the worksheet during times in their schedule that occur regularly, such as their commute or their young child's nap time. (Some may argue that worrying during a commute is dangerous, but people are likely to worry during that time anyway and they are likely to be less anxious if they are focused on problem-solving instead.) If the client doesn't have such a time that is at least 15 minutes long, help them to plan a time to coincide with an event, such as before they brush their teeth, after lunch, or during a short commute and then continuing after they get home.

When clients are worrying about a specific event, such as relatives visiting, a speech, moving, or a wedding, the second worksheet (p. 26) is indicated. The point to this worksheet is to postpone the worry until the client begins planning for the event. For complex tasks, such as a decision about college or planning a wedding, you may want to help the client break down the steps involved. Once the two of you have decided upon the steps, you can set goal dates for beginning to address each step, then the client can postpone the worry until that step shows up in their calendar or they can remind themselves "I'll worry about that on September 15th," for example.

An important role for you is to help your client briefly accept, or "taste," worries that arise outside the designated periods and use strategies to let go of the thought. Practicing self-control desensitization in sessions with the client will help them to let go of worries, images, and physical symptoms of anxiety more readily (see p. 151-153 in the Therapists' Guide) as part of the postponement process. Knowing they will address the worry later usually helps them to release it now. Achieving this involves a simple three-step process: (1) "tasting" the thought, (2) reminding themselves that they'll think about it during the worry and problem-solving session, then (3) using a brief strategy or two to release it. A lovely metaphor for this process that you can teach your clients is as follows: When a worry comes to mind, think of it like a car driving down your street; you watch it come and go, but you're not going to become a passenger.

Being in the Now:
Mindfulness

If you are like most therapists, you already engage clients in the practice of mindfulness. If not, the workbook will be helpful. Consider looking at Chapter 7, particularly the walking exercises, even if you currently use mindfulness.

One of the most useful things to remember about mindfulness is that clients who have attention-deficit/ hyperactivity disorder (ADHD) or whose worries are extreme will likely have difficulty being able to maintain focus in the moment. When this is the case, it may be necessary to add stimulation. Going on a walk, engaging in yard-work, or even adding stimulation into the session (e.g., a scented candle, incense, instrumental music, or a nature recording) may be indicated. Ironically, adding stimulation can help to calm the mind because it can help clients with attentional problems from getting bored and it can help to distract excessively worried clients.

Weather permitting, you can ask clients to consider taking a mindful walk with you. If, after you explain the implications of privacy on a walk together, they are comfortable being seen with you in public, you may proceed. If they have concerns, make sure they know this is *not* necessary. If they aren't concerned or otherwise decide to proceed, decide what they'd like for you to do should one of you see someone you know. See pages 30–31 of the client workbook for a script for going on a walk as well as the follow-up walk exercises. Alternatively, listen to the free recording of the mindfulness walk to get even more ideas about what to say while walking with a client. If they aren't comfortable going for a walk with you, between sessions they can use the recording or self-guide their walk with the script.

Particularly with perfectionistic clients, explain that the average person has over 2,000 thoughts per hour, so it's unrealistic to expect to take a 15-minute walk (over 500 thoughts on average) without any unwanted thoughts seeping through. Giving clients permission to have unwanted thoughts interfere will increase the likelihood that they will be able to free themselves from those thoughts. Encourage them to accept the thoughts when they have them, taste them (briefly think them), then gently shift to the moment, focusing on the present like a baby would.

After about 10 minutes on the walk, sitting outside or inside, assess how they did being in the moment. If they are unhappy with how it went or you believe they were not focusing on the moment for a significant percentage of the time, assist with labeling their senses. This is explained in walk 5 of the client portion of the workbook (p. 31). Clients don't usually need this step; however, when they do, help them to think of labeling as a bridge to being mindful. When the client finds it very difficult to stay in the moment, labeling their experiences will get them in the moment. When indicated, demonstrate this by labeling your sensory experiences on a walk with the client. Use brief labels over lengthy ones (e.g., "green grass," "feeling the breeze," "hearing the breeze," "seeing it move the trees," "sound of our feet," "smell of a barbecue," "blue sky," "white clouds"). Explain to the client that once their labeling has successfully placed them in the moment, they can let go of the labels, focusing on their senses like a baby would. When thoughts derail them, encourage them to allow the thought, "taste" the thought (think it briefly), then gently move back to the moment without labeling. Use labeling as needed.

Depending upon the client, you can refer to the labeling process as a game. The objective is not to be worry free. Rather, the objectives are: (1) when unwanted thoughts interfere, catch them early; (2) "taste" the thoughts before shifting to the moment; (3) use the labeling as a bridge to being in the moment when needed; (4) spend more time focusing on the raw sensations without words; and (5) spend less time actively worrying. Focusing on the raw sensations like a baby would is best, but labeling one's senses is more relaxing than worrying and can provide a transition to being in the moment without the labels.

Better-But-Believable Thinking

Many therapists practice cognitive therapy, even if it is just to offer an alternative perspective. Certainly, our thoughts affect how we feel, so it makes sense to think more positively. However, if we suggest to our clients to "think positive," they may reach for the most positive thought they can think. You may have made the same error in failed attempts to help your clients' depression or anxiety. The problem is that, if the client doesn't really believe that the thought is true, it's likely to be useless. As a result, clients often give up hope and stop trying to change their thinking.

If we reach for the expert advice of famous cognitive therapists such as Aaron Beck (1967), Albert Ellis (1975), and David Burns (1980), cognitive therapy can be quite complex. Clients are first expected to identify the thought or thoughts causing their depression or anxiety. The next step clients are expected to do is identify the thought style. Are they *catastrophizing*, *global labelling*, *emotionally reasoning*, *mind reading*, or another thought style? This is further complicated when clients' thoughts fit more than one thought style or when they have difficulty deciding which thought style applies. Once they have decided which thought style they are thinking, they are instructed to look in the portion of the book where the expert author offers advice on finding the antidote to each thought style, or they must try to remember their therapist's advice for each thought style. Finally, they construct a new thought. The result is that this laborious process can increase stress. Depressed clients may find it difficult to get motivated to go through the process. Finally, the time commitment involved can cause the client to abandon their efforts.

To fix these problems with cognitive therapy, it occurred to me that a simpler process would improve both compliance and effectiveness. I also realized that it is much better to think of a believable, neutral thought that is better than the depressing or anxiety-producing thought—even if it isn't particularly positive. In addition, I use a Socratic approach, which is an advantage over more directive approaches. Finally, I created a catchy, memorable approach: "better-but-believable thoughts" (B^3s) (Abel, 2010).

The new approach is to ask clients when they are feeling stressed, depressed, or otherwise distressed: "What is something that is better but believable?" A similar way to think of this type of thinking is that when clients are worried or thinking negative thoughts that lead to depression, it's like wearing poop-colored glasses, and we see everything as being worse than it is in reality. With B^3s, instead of replacing the poop-colored glasses with rose-colored glasses, we replace them with clear glasses. We see reality; we see truth. In addition, we can choose to focus on the more positive side of reality rather than focusing on the negative.

When clients create B^3s, you may find them wording positive B^3s in a negative direction. For instance, a client's B^3s might be: "There's less than a 5% chance I will fail the test" or "It's unlikely my girlfriend is cheating on me." In these examples, they are still thinking of failing the test and thinking about an unfaithful girlfriend. They may even visualize their failure by seeing an "F" written at the top of the exam, or have images of catching their girlfriend cheating on them with another person. Therefore, when you find B^3s for clients, word them in a positive direction and help your clients to do the same. In these two examples, better B^3s are:

"There's a greater than 95% chance I'll pass the test and at least an 80% chance it will be an A or a B," and "It's likely my girlfriend is being faithful."

Because we know that worry and anxiety interfere with problem-solving, they may also interfere with clients' ability to be creative about finding B^3s. People who suffer from GAD do tend to think myopically rather than creatively. Helping clients to use relaxation before generating B^3s can be helpful. I also recommend that you and your client independently think of B^3s first, because the creativity literature indicates that we arrive at a better and more complete list if we work independently first, rather than brainstorming together. Once you have run out of ideas and your client has stopped writing, ask them if they'd like to read their list first or read your list first. Then have them rate each B^3 on a scale from 2 to 10, with 2 indicating the thought is not very helpful and 10 indicating it is very helpful. Be sure to ask the client to rate your ideas honestly as opposed to being concerned about hurting your feelings about your ideas. Then choose two to four helpful thoughts. If the items are very similar in content, consider combining them or eliminating them even when they are highly rated, especially if there are other items that help in a different way. Keep the items that address a different favorable aspect, even if the ratings are a little lower. For instance, let's say your client has the following list and ratings around the fear of their son getting hurt playing football.

- He wears a helmet: 7
- His brother played for five years with no serious injury: 8
- He is a very tough kid: 7
- He really loves to play: 6
- He plays with friends: 3
- It's better than playing video games: 4
- He's getting exercise: 6

In this example, eliminate the B^3s in the list that are rated as 3 or 4 because there are clearly several better options. It might be tempting to choose the three highest rated B^3s. However, because the first three are safety-related items, it may be best to choose only the highest rated B^3 ("His brother played for five years with no serious injury") out of these three. The rationale for eliminating the relatively highly rated safety items is two-fold. First, if we have too many items, the list can become cumbersome. Second, given that "He really loves to play" and "He's getting exercise" are not safety related, are quite different from one another, and are moderately helpful, it's better to use them than the higher rated safety items about the helmet and him being tough.

Perhaps your most important role with clients and B^3s is to help them think outside the box. For example, in the above situation, because the fear is that he'll get hurt, a client may only think about alternative thoughts that are safety related. It's important for you to think of all aspects of the situation, not just those that are in direct opposition to the worry. You can be a good model by using more creative B^3s. You may also want to have a conversation with your client about their son and football. Asking them the right questions may help them to come up with some better B^3s. Alternatively, to help them think more on their own, just encourage them to think of all thoughts about their son playing football that are better thoughts than "he's going to get hurt." Some possibilities for better B^3s: "He's always in a good mood when he comes home from football practice and games," "He has a good relationship with the coach," "Playing football makes him stronger," and "He will study harder because of the school's requirement to maintain a B average to stay on the football team."

Stop Should-ing on Yourself

The words that we use affect how we feel. When clients tell themselves that they "need" to do something, whether it's their inner dialogue or something they say aloud, they often feel a great deal of pressure or anxiety. We all use at least some of these imperatives: "should," "need to," "have to," "must," and "gotta." In small doses, the use of these words is fine. However, with many clients these words are overused and cause excessive stress. The main problem with these imperatives is that they imply there is no choice when there is almost always a choice.

As a therapist, it's useful to be mindful of whether your client uses these words sparingly and accurately or whether they overuse these words and use them inaccurately such that it is increasing their anxiety and depression.

If you overuse these words yourself, you may not readily notice when others overuse them. You may not be aware if you overuse them. If in doubt, get feedback from people close to you and consider using the client workbook portion for yourself, both for your own mental health and to be a healthy model for your clients.

When you determine that such imperatives are likely adding significantly to a client's stress, your next role is to gently point out the frequency and effect on the client. Consider tallying the number of times the client uses these words and then saying something like this:

> In the first 30 minutes of our session, I tallied the number of times you said "I need to" or "I should" and it was 42 times! Using these words is probably putting a lot of pressure on you. I'm wondering how much the use of these words is contributing to your anxiety. I also wonder whether they are contributing to your depression if you feel that you have been failing to do these things.

Behind nearly all imperatives there is a "want to," even if that "want to" is only to avoid consequences or get something checked off a list. Help clients find the "want tos" behind their "shoulds." Most people agree that when they find a reason that they "want" to do something it does two things. First, it decreases tension and anxiety. Second, it increases motivation.

For example:

Therapist: For most things that we *feel* we need to do or should do, there is a "want." For instance, you said you need to wash your car today. Do you *want* your car to be clean?
Client: I do.
Therapist: Would you be willing to try saying, "I want my car to be clean?"
Client: I want my car to be clean. Hmm?
Therapist: How are you feeling about washing your car?
Client: Better! I'm visualizing my car clean now and I like it! I really don't like my car to be dirty and I know I'll feel better once my car is clean.

Here are some questions you could ask clients to help them find their "want tos."

- Will you feel better after you've done it?
- What is the benefit of doing it?
- Are there additional benefits of doing it?
- What will happen if you don't do it?
- Could you do it another time?
- Could you do something else instead?
- Is there a compromise?

Consider brainstorming possible "want tos" and "coulds" and picking the best ones, as was demonstrated with B³s in the previous chapter. For example, some "want tos" with the car: "I want to be outdoors," "I want the exercise," "I'll enjoy practicing mindfulness while washing the car," "I'll feel a sense of accomplishment," and "I want my car to be clean." Examples of "coulds": "I could pay my teenager to wash it," "I could go to a car wash," "I could go to the self-service car wash with the wands," "I could let the car be dirty," and "I could do it tomorrow." Then ask the client to say their original statement aloud while noticing how it feels. Do the same with the new statement.

Therapist: Let's try the old and new statements to see how they feel. First say "I need to wash my car" while noticing how it feels.
Client: I need to wash my car.
Therapist: Now say the new statement while noticing the difference in how you feel.
Client: I'm going to wash my car tomorrow, when I'll have more time to do it mindfully. I want to spend some active time outside and I want my car to be clean.
Therapist: Feel different?
Client: Yes! I'm less stressed and kind of looking forward to making time to do this tomorrow.

Many people who put pressure on themselves do the same with loved ones. They tell their spouses, children, and even friends that they *should* do this or they *need* to do that. Sometimes it's easier for clients to begin to change their imperative habit with others than with themselves. The process is similar, but the client may feel irritated rather than stressed. Their friends, family, and colleagues will likely feel stressed.

In fact, they probably learned this habit from someone who placed these imperatives on them, likely a parent but sometimes teachers, coaches, or other family members. Often these words and phrases are used in an attempt to motivate children. While they can often be motivators, they can also be stressors. If your client remembers how it felt when they were younger and on the receiving end of these words and phrases, this may motivate them to change. These are sometimes the same people who have become perfectionistic. Therefore "Perfectionism" (Chapter 23) may be helpful too.

Whether their "should-ing" is aimed at themselves or others, help clients to identify people in their lives who can help increase their awareness of their use of imperatives. In addition, discuss how they would like to ask others to tell them when they notice them "should-ing" on themselves or someone else. One possibility is to repeat the imperative word or words like a question—that is, saying "*need to?*" going up in pitch with the word "to." Another is to gently ask, "What is the want?" Finally, a gesture may be preferred, such as having the helper touch their nose or gently placing a hand on the client's shoulder. In session, you can hold up a sticky note to simultaneously remind the client to use a relaxation or mindfulness strategy while making them aware of saying words such as "need to."

Finally, if these strategies prove ineffective and your client can identify where they learned these behaviors, talking about these memories and processing associated emotions may be helpful. Chapter 11 can help with this.

Everything in Moderation:
Avoid the Extremes

Extreme words and imperatives are similar. Therefore, some of the same strategies you used in the previous chapter can be used with extremes. Whether extreme words are thoughts or are spoken, when clients use them they can cause problems. Because we feel how we think, depression, anxiety, anger, and frustration can set in when clients use these negative extreme words.

Your goal as a therapist is two-fold when it comes to changing the habit of using extreme words. First, it is to gently point out the issue, much in the same way that was discussed with imperatives in the previous chapter. Second, it is to find the exceptions. You can work Socratically or point out the exceptions directly. For instance, if a client states, "I never do anything right," you could ask them what they did right today. Or you could say something like, "You were here on time and you arrived safely. So you got ready on time and must have driven right."

A great example is when clients say, "I'm having a bad day. Everything has gone wrong." After empathizing that you are sorry they are having a frustrating day and asking them what happened, you can begin to point out the exceptions. You could encourage them to think about everything that went right. Even if it's something little, like they didn't have to wait at a certain stoplight that is often long. They made it to work on time. They had hot water. Their car started. They arrived safely. Maybe you can challenge them to think of one thing that went right today. Maybe there was something they learned? Was there something that made them laugh or smile?

When you feel like your day is bad, you stop seeing the good in it and will miss positive things. Encourage your client to consider the following:

- If you didn't have difficult days, you wouldn't appreciate the easier and better ones as much.
- You probably learn more from the difficult days than from the easy ones.
- When you are having "one of those days," do something nice for yourself or, even better, do something nice for someone else. Maybe do both!
- Sometimes things that at first seem bad end up being great. Like the people who met when they got into a car wreck and ended up getting married. Or like my friend who lost his job and ended up getting a job he liked much better that is way closer to home.
- When you feel like you're having a bad day, look at how many hours you have left for it to change.
- Look forward to tomorrow being a better day.
- Remember the Serenity Prayer (see Chapter 16)—especially "accept the things you cannot change."
- Make a list of all the exceptions to "nothing is going right." List the things that could have gone wrong and didn't.

Therapist Chapter 11 | Acceptance of Healthy Emotion

As a therapist, you certainly understand the difference between, on the one hand, healthy emotion and, on the other, false alarms in anxiety and negative thinking in depression. We do not want to help clients repress healthy emotion. Rather than trying to relieve healthy emotions with coping strategies designed to let go of them, we want to encourage emotional processing in at least two ways. The first is to help clients identify and accept healthy emotion about current and recent events, as outlined in Chapter 11. The second is to consider unlocking unresolved emotion from prior traumatic events. This can be particularly useful if clients are not responding to cognitive–behavioral therapy (CBT) and mindfulness therapy.

While there are mountains of empirical evidence supporting the use of CBT in the treatment of anxiety and depression, GAD clients who suppress emotional processing are less likely to benefit (Borkovec et al., 2002). In one study, depressed clients who experienced more emotions during the process of therapy fared better with CBT than those who did less emotional processing (Castonguay et al., 1996).

People with GAD feel more threatened by, and perceive greater discomfort from, emotions than controls (Llera & Newman, 2010). Furthermore, their attempts to control emotion may lead to increased hyper-vigilance and more labile emotions (Newman, Castonguay, Borkovec, & Molnar, 2004). Interestingly, individuals with GAD may use worry as a coping strategy to suppress more painful memories, as evidenced by Borkovec and Roemer (1995). In their study, students who worried to a healthy degree were compared to students meeting criteria for GAD. Those with GAD were significantly more likely to endorse the item "Worrying about most of the things I worry about is a way to distract myself from worrying about even more emotional things, things that I don't want to think about." For a more extensive review of the literature on emotional processing, GAD, and to some degree depression, see Newman et al. (2011).

Therapies to encourage emotional processing are beyond the scope of this book. Use skills that you know to help clients process emotions. These may include re-parenting in schema therapy (Young, Klosko, & Weishaar, 2006), experiential therapies (e.g., open chair), movement therapy, or diaries aimed at recording emotional experiences. Even reflective listening has been shown to lead to significantly higher levels of emotional processing than CBT alone (Borkovec & Costello, 1993).

Marsha Linehan (1993) identified primary emotions (healthy emotion) and secondary emotions (unhealthy emotion in response to primary emotions), as seen in Chapter 11. In addition to using CBT strategies, your role is to help clients access, identify, accept, and express primary emotion. When this is done effectively, secondary emotions may resolve. Otherwise, use coping strategies for both secondary emotions and other unhealthy reactions to events such as depressing irrational thoughts and worry about the future.

Relaxation and Making Recordings

The relaxation procedure that may be the most effective is progressive relaxation, sometimes referred to as progressive muscle relaxation, in which one systematically tenses and releases 16 muscle groups in the body. This is particularly useful if the client suffers from insomnia, muscle tension, and/or tension headaches. It has also been found useful in treating a wide array of other issues, from premenstrual symptoms to fatigue to chronic pain. Many therapists have learned to teach progressive relaxation, but most haven't learned to do it properly. Teaching you how to properly train clients to learn progressive relaxation is beyond the scope of the client workbook. If you do not take at least 50 minutes to teach the first session and use at least three subsequent sessions to combine muscle groups, teach recall, and teach differential relaxation, it is recommended that you either watch my 90-minute webinar (Abel, 2016) or read the most recent training manual (Bernstein, Borkovec, & Hazlett-Stevens, 2000) to learn to teach clients progressive relaxation properly.

The remainder of this chapter will focus on other forms of relaxation. You can read the scripts from Chapter 12 to your clients. Feel free to change and embellish these scripts or create your own. Remember to use the advice in Therapist Chapter 3 when guiding relaxation. In summary, speak slowly, use process words, pause, and vary the pitch of your voice. You may also purchase the supplemental relaxation recordings at AnxietyStLouisPsychologist. com/free or create your own recordings.

If you would like to create your own recordings and have a PC, go to Audacityteam.org, where you can download Audacity. It is a free and powerful recording studio. It's relatively easy to learn as it works very much like a tape recorder. If you have difficulty, it is recommended that you go to YouTube and watch training videos or use the tutorials on the Audacity website. To convert your recording to an MP3 so that you may send it to a client, go to Lame.buanzo.org. A restart of your computer is necessary to begin using it with Audacity.

If you have a Mac, iPad, or iPhone, you have GarageBand. Double click or tap on the guitar icon to open it. If it's not in your dock, open it from your Applications folder. Much like Audacity, it's intuitive, but there are free workshops available at the Apple stores, videos on Apple.com, and several beginner training videos on YouTube.

Once you have completed recording, choose "Share" from the menu and then choose "Send Song to iTunes." In iTunes, choose "File" then "Convert" and at the bottom of the list you will see "Create MP3 Version." If you do not see "Create MP3 Version" in the menu, choose iTunes > Preferences, click "General," and click "Import Settings." At the top of that pop-up, you will see "Import Using." Choose "MP3 Encoder." Now go back to File > Convert > Create MP3 Version. If this procedure has changed after an upgrade of iTunes, under iTunes Help, search "create MP3 version" or look to iTunes or YouTube.

In lieu of creating an MP3, you can make a recording onto a disk or a flash drive. If you do choose to create MP3s, it's not recommended that you send these rather large files directly via email. Instead use Box.com or Dropbox.com. You can upload your files to these free sites and then send a link to clients for them to download the recordings to their devices. They will usually download them and play on iTunes. You can also make recordings for clients on their own smart phone.

About 10% of clients experience a paradoxical response to relaxation such that attempts to help them relax actually make them feel more anxious. This may result from performance anxiety, such that trying to "do it right" creates anxiety or simply trying to relax creates tension. Others may get frustrated when they don't immediately feel better. Using process words can reduce performance tension for some clients. Using the phrase "making no effort to relax" prior to relaxation patter can be helpful, as well. For example, "Making no effort to relax, just allowing each breath you exhale to loosen your body."

For some clients, relaxing makes them feel more vulnerable, thereby increasing a false sense of threat. This is particularly common among survivors of trauma who feel, and often believe, that they must be on guard to be safe. When a feeling of vulnerability raises anxiety, proceeding with open eyes and even starting by using relaxation on a walk are likely to make them feel safer. Furthermore, if a client feels threatened by mindfulness, I recommend a Socratic approach: "Do you think you are safer when you are inside your head worrying or do you think you are safer when you're focusing on what you see and hear?" Clients usually realize that they are safer when noticing what they see and hear. Once the client is comfortable relaxing quietly with their eyes open, begin relaxation with eyes open and say something like, "Feeling free to close your eyes when you'd like, knowing you can open them again at any time."

Finally, it may take time for the client to build trust with you before they are able to allow themselves to be vulnerable enough to benefit from relaxation with you. Also, as they work through their trauma, they may feel safer to use relaxation with you.

Nip the Worry Spiral in the Bud:
Applied Relaxation and Self-Control Desensitization

Worry and anxiety occur in a spiral of interactions between thoughts, images, physical sensations, and emotions. If your client is already practicing coping strategies, you may encourage them to read Chapter 13 first. Mindful observation, labeling, and acceptance can work regardless of where your client is in the spiral. However, relaxation strategies and cognitive therapy are usually of limited use, and can even add to a client's distress, once the spiral is out of control. In fact, early studies using cognitive therapy and relaxation therapy to treat GAD were disappointing until Borkovec and Costello (1993) recognized the importance of catching the anxiety spiral early. Once they developed applied relaxation and self-control desensitization (SCD) for the treatment of worry, GAD treatment became much more successful. In short, applied relaxation is about teaching clients to use relaxation throughout the day to prevent anxiety from getting out of control, while SCD is a way for clients to repeatedly practice catching anxiety early in the spiral, thereby weakening the spiral right there in the session.

Applied Relaxation
Your role with applied relaxation to help clients maintain relaxation throughout the therapy session and encourage them to use the same principles outside of the session on a daily basis in everyday life. In the session, start with an explanation that you are going to help them maintain relaxation throughout the session, so you'd like to begin the session with relaxation. If they are eager to share something to "get it off their chest" or seek your advice, allow them to do so, but suggest that you discuss it after they've done some relaxation. However, postpone this activity if your client recently got particularly bad news or experienced a traumatic event. Remember that we don't want to help our clients repress healthy emotions.

Once you conclude that your client is relaxed, review the usefulness of maintaining relaxation throughout the day by using frequent application of meditation and relaxation. Explain that you are going to help them to practice that skill in the session today by periodically holding up a sticky note as a gentle reminder to continue using coping strategies.

Choose any simple form of relaxation or mindfulness that they have learned and ask them to engage in that skill each time you raise your hand holding the sticky note. Hold up the sticky note every minute or two. Also, if you see that your client is getting anxious (e.g., furrowed brow, tapping feet or fingers), you can hold up the note.

About 10 minutes later, switch the form of relaxation. You can also use observation or acceptance if that has been helpful for the client in the past. Try to use at least three different forms of relaxation or acceptance. When using any form of breathing as relaxation, only hold up the sticky note when the client is not talking.

If the client stops talking when you hold up the sticky note, remind them that the goal is to maintain relaxation throughout the day without stopping their flow of activity. Explain that if they feel like they need to stop every time they notice a sticky note, it will likely be counterproductive and annoying to the point where they may stop using the notes, or other reminders, like changing the text tone on their smart phone.

About 10 minutes before the conclusion of the session, ask your client which strategy worked the best. Consider putting the sticky note right behind you or wearing it on your chest after that. Then ask your client to use their favorite strategy when they notice it.

At the conclusion of the session, it's useful to give them at least a dozen of the sticky notes you used in the session for them to use for applied relaxation outside the session. By the end of the session, they will have already begun a habit of using their coping strategy with that color and size. Furthermore, they will be more likely to remember to put them up if they see them in their pocket or purse. Finally, because you gave the sticky notes to them, they will be more likely to value them than ones they might get from home or their office.

As a supplement to the use of sticky notes, Chapter 13 contains a list of other ways clients can remind themselves. You may be able to help tailor those cues to the individual. If there is something they do frequently or something that you know is stressful, you may be able to develop cues for them. For instance, have smokers change their lighter or place a sticky note in their cigarette pack. Have a courier change their keyring, put a sticky on their dash, or hang something from their rearview mirror. If you have a client taking medication that makes them thirsty, have them put a colorful hairband or rubber band around their glass and add a sticky note in the restroom. If a client is stressed by their boss, use the boss as a cue to relax. When they see their boss walking down the hall, this will act as a cue to help them to get into the habit to use a strategy before engaging. When they see that the boss is calling them or see an email alert, they can use strategies prior to answering the call or opening the email.

Ask clients each session how many times they are using mini-relaxations throughout the day. The goal is to apply relaxation at least 20 times per day and preferably 30–50 times per day. It may be helpful to remind them that they can apply relaxation without stopping or otherwise interfering with their flow of activity. Demonstrate this in the session. For example:

> *I'm talking to you and you're listening. We can both be thinking of the surfaces beneath us as sponges without stopping the flow of our conversation. You can be focusing on the feeling of your breathing and continue to listen. No matter what we are doing, we can use some form of relaxation or acceptance without interfering with our flow of activity.*

Have clients bring in their self-monitoring form and note the number of times they indicate that that they are applying the strategies. If their anxiety is above a 3 and the estimated number of times they applied the strategies is under 20, review and problem-solve. Help them to add or change reminders and review that they needn't take time to use the strategies.

Self-Control Desensitization

Self-control desensitization is a way to help clients repeatedly catch their worry and anxiety spirals early. In some cases, this may apply to frustration and anger as well. You should notice a weakening of the anxiety spiral within 10 minutes, but I recommend a longer session. When used with anxiety, begin with a rationale to your client that will go something like this:

> *We've talked a great deal about the anxiety spiral and the importance of catching your anxiety early. Today we are going to weaken your anxiety spiral and strengthen your habit of catching it early in the session. First, I will guide you through relaxation. After you appear to be deeply relaxed, I will introduce things that I expect will trigger some anxiety. However, don't wait until you feel anxious. Instead, as soon as you feel a little less relaxed, I'd like for you*

to raise your index finger [demonstrate by keeping your hand on your leg and lifting only your index finger a little]. Hold up your finger until you feel completely relaxed again and then lower it [demonstrate your finger completely relaxing on your leg]. For instance, if after you get very relaxed, you consider yourself to be at a 2 on a 0–10 scale, when you feel you are at a 2.1 raise your finger. In all likelihood, your level will go higher than that, but the idea is to nip this spiral in the bud repeatedly. This will provide you with a great deal of practice letting go early in the spiral before your anxiety gets out of control.

Begin with relaxation that has worked for the client in the past. Remember, the goal of SCD is to prevent anxiety from getting out of control. Therefore, it's useful to check to see whether the client is relaxed by getting a level (e.g., 0–10) before introducing a worry, image, or physical sensation of anxiety. If their anxiety is still high, use a combination of acceptance and coping strategies to get them down below a 4. If they are unable to relax, it is best that SCD is postponed to another session. Once the client is relaxed, bring up a worry, an image of a feared event, or an anxiety symptom (e.g., heaviness in chest, tension in neck). The instant they raise their finger, even if you are mid-sentence, begin using relaxation patter, acceptance strategies, or cognitive therapy. Repeat the process. The following are the steps that I suggest:

1. Provide the rationale for SCD and explain the process.
2. Ask your client to support their head and neck against the chair, the couch, or a pillow and close their eyes. Begin relaxation patter.
3. Determine their anxiety level. If it is 4 or above, continue with more relaxation. If the client is unable to get relaxed, reschedule SCD for another time. Proceed when the client is relaxed.
4. Introduce an anxiety-producing stimulus.
5. Once they raise their finger, begin acceptance and/or relaxation patter.
6. Once they lower their finger, repeat steps 4–6 until 7.
7. Your client has either taken much longer to raise their finger after the anxiety-producing stimulus is presented *or* they have lowered their finger rapidly. Once you observe the anxiety weakening, create a challenge. A challenge can be created in at least three ways. One way is to make the worry or image more negative or otherwise more anxiety-producing. Another way is to combine a physical sensation with either a worry or imagery. In the third option, when using imagery and if the client has succeeded in quickly letting go, reintroduce the image and, instead of letting go of it, have them continue to visualize the stressful event while continuing the relaxation.
8. Finally, once they are letting go easily, you can shift the responsibility to the client. When their finger goes up, simply say "letting go on your own" or something similar.

Encourage your client to practice SCD on their own, pointing out that there is no need for them to raise their finger at home.

If your client doesn't get anxious despite presenting multiple triggers and presenting the worst imaginable outcome for their worry, they might be accepting, they may be so relaxed that they can't get anxious or they may have become conditioned to relax with the thoughts or images. I recommend that you say something like this: "Noticing that when you're in a relaxed state, these worries do not bother you." Once you ask them to open their eyes, you can explore whether they were accepting and encourage them to use this strategy along with relaxation in the future.

Improving Compliance
Encourage your clients to use the "Daily Self-Monitoring 2" worksheet in Chapter 11 to keep track of how often they are using their strategies. Ask them to bring in the form. "I didn't have time" is clients' most frequently

stated reason that they didn't use the strategies more frequently during the day. Clients frequently forget that they can engage in these strategies without stopping their flow of activity. The in-session demonstration of applied relaxation at the beginning of this chapter is helpful to reinforce that fact. Other reasons include, "I forgot" or "I didn't notice the reminders." When this is the case, help them to add or change reminders. Consider asking them to take their smartphone out and make the changes in the session. Also consider giving them a different-colored sticky note.

Another reason that clients state "I didn't need it." If their ratings for anxiety and irritability are from 0 to 2 with an occasional 3, they are right. They don't need it. Determine what number is just enough energy to be very productive yet relaxed—exactly where we want to be most of the time. You can also define this for the client as being a 2. If, prior to therapy, the client was about a 6 or 7 most of the time, with frequent increases to 8 or 9 (for example), they may feel they don't need to relax if they are at a 4 or a 5. Encourage your client to aim for being at a 2 most of the time. Consider this rationale:

> *If you're at a 4, you're probably not particularly concerned about your anxiety. It's much better than where you used to be and you don't feel particularly stressed. However, if you are at a 4 and something stressful happens, it may easily send you up to a 7 or an 8. If the same thing were to happen when you're at a 2, it may not bother you at all. Or you may be able to catch it early and rapidly reduce it back to a 2, or you might only go up to a 5 or 6. Because it doesn't take any time, it's good to use your strategies unless you're already down to a "2 or 3."*

Positive Psychology

Similar to B³s (see Therapist Chapter 8), positive psychology is viewing life in a positive way. Positive psychology differs from cognitive therapy in that it can apply to everyone and is not necessarily aimed at treating depression. A pitfall of using positive psychology with clients is being so positive that empathy is lacking, running the risk of alienating the client. Therefore, remember to support clients' feelings and avoid "sugar-coating" their experiences. Once you have supported them, help them in a way that is similar by using the "Yin and Yang" worksheet. That is, find something positive that is related to *almost* everything that is troubling them. Avoid trying to point out the yang in a fresh trauma and perhaps never do so for certain traumas (e.g., rape, loss of a child).

If your client has low self-esteem, it will be necessary to help them with the "Gratitudes" worksheet, which is about positive things in their life, especially their personal attributes. Point out the attributes that you see in them and if they are internal attributes, be sure to back them up with examples. If they are external, ask whether anyone else has told them the same thing. If the client does not believe them to be true at all, don't list them. Seeing a positive attribute that they don't think they possess may backfire. Looking at that attribute and believing they don't have it may make them feel worse. Do list it if they believe it is partially true as they may "grow into it."

If they forget to do their gratitudes, you may suggest that they put a sheet of paper in their underwear drawer, or somewhere else that they will see it daily (e.g., by their toothbrush). Sometimes clients can benefit from a Socratic approach to gratitudes based on prior conversations you've had about good things in their life. For example, if you remember them saying positive things about their relationship with their sister Elizabeth, you could ask, "Are you grateful for Elizabeth?"

Removing the Crutches

Operant conditioning is the learning that occurs when an individual's behavior is modified by its consequences. With anxiety and depression, we frequently see clients develop habits that help them in the short term but exacerbate, or at least maintain, their problems in the long run. We can call these behaviors "crutches." Usually, we see crutches become habitual through negative reinforcement and positive reinforcement, mostly the former. There is a great deal of confusion about these terms and how they operate in the crutches clients develop when attempting to manage their depression and anxiety.

As noted in Chapter 15, "positive" refers to adding a stimulus while "negative" refers to removing a stimulus. "Reinforcement" refers to increasing a behavior, while "punishment" refers to decreasing a behavior. Below is a chart that shows these mechanisms of operant conditioning with an example of each type.

	Apply a Stimulus (+)	**Remove a Stimulus (−)**
Increases Behavior	*Positive Reinforcement* Jonathan feels a good buzz after taking a few hits off his bong. Therefore, he uses it more often.	*Negative Reinforcement* Jonathan's anxiety goes away after taking a few hits off his bong. So the next time he's anxious, he uses it again. Tori feels anxious at a party, so she leaves. She is relieved, but more scared to go to a party the next time and avoids it altogether.
Decreases Behavior	*Positive Punishment* Jenny drives the speed limit after getting a speeding ticket. Her speeding behavior is punished.	*Negative Punishment* Ethan and Riley fight less while playing games after their Xbox is taken away for a day as a result of their fighting.

Note that Jonathan's use of marijuana is both positively and negatively reinforced. He is positively reinforced by the positive feeling of being high, which increases his use in the future. And, because his anxiety goes away from smoking, he uses it the next time he feels anxious. In anxiety and depression, we commonly see alcohol use, use of benzodiazepines (e.g., clonazepam/Klonopin, alprazolam/Xanax, lorazepam/Ativan, or diazepam/Valium), and use of prescription painkillers, usually opiates. Use of other addictive substances (e.g., cocaine, heroin) is sometimes present as well. Benzodiazepines are used more frequently among individuals with anxiety and those with mixed anxiety and depression, rather than those suffering from depression alone.

When a client behaves in such a way as to avoid, reduce, or escape anxiety, that behavior is likely to do two things: (1) increase those avoidance and escape behaviors and (2) increase the anxiety associated with facing the feared stimulus or worry. Furthermore, when a client realizes they are out of control, it contributes to depression and they may gain weight, spend a lot of money, or feel incapable of managing without drugs or alcohol. Finally, most of the substances that clients use to self-medicate not only negatively and positively reinforce anxiety, but are also depressants that often contribute to depression.

Unfortunately, when attempting to comfort clients, many therapists negatively reinforce their clients' anxiety. By giving reassurance or encouraging any number of negatively-reinforcing behaviors, you may inadvertently increase clients' fear and anxiety. This is a natural response. Therapists don't generally encourage the use of illicit drugs or alcohol, but they do commonly encourage the use of prescription drugs. While many medications like SSRIs can be very helpful for treating depression and anxiety, quick acting medications like benzodiazepenes are usually problematic, especially Xanax. Therapists want to help their clients feel better, not make them feel worse. Yet, in the long run, the temporary comfort that is provided may serve to maintain and even strengthen the discomfort. Many therapists increase anxiety by encouraging clients to engage in behaviors that negatively reinforce their anxiety.

For example, let's say that Henry feels pressure in his chest and is fearful of having a heart attack. When he has this fear, he feels compelled to check his heart rate to make sure it is beating consistently. He also reassures himself that his doctor has run every test imaginable and that he is fine. While these behaviors temporarily reduce his anxiety, he quickly rebounds with the thought: "What if the doctor missed something?" He then checks his heart rate again. This cycle may repeat for several minutes or even hours, "ping-ponging" back and forth between anxious thoughts and feelings on the one hand, quickly followed by reassuring thoughts and checking his heart on the other hand. Each time he engages in this cycle, he negatively reinforces both the anxiety and the urge to self-reassure and check his heart. His therapist may try to use what they think is cognitive therapy by reassuring him and encouraging him to check his heart rate:

> *Henry, your heart is fine. All your test results indicate that your heart is strong. You can stop worrying about your heart, because your doctors have reassured you that you have a clean bill of health. I'm sure your doctors didn't miss anything. And if checking your heart helps you to feel better maybe it would be helpful for you to check your pulse longer in the future and let your anxiety reduce more before you pull your finger off your pulse. Use your breathing exercises to help calm you as well. Also, if you think it would make you feel better to get a second opinion from a doctor, go ahead and do that. I know it's only your anxiety, but if it will help to reduce your anxiety to repeat the tests with another physician, by all means do that.*

The therapist in this script is trying to reassure Henry and get him to see that there is nothing wrong with his heart. However, reassurance is not just ineffective with individuals who worry that something is wrong with their body, it usually negatively reinforces it. Hearing the above might make Henry feel better for a few minutes or even for as long as a day or two. Nonetheless, in situations like this, the anxiety is maintained or is even exacerbated in the long run. Seeing a physician for a repeat of the test or a second opinion is often helpful for a week or two, but it also typically becomes negatively-reinforcing as well. Of course, sometimes a second opinion is warranted and can be helpful.

It is alright to just once tell the client that you don't believe they have anything to worry about or state that you believe their anxiety is the problem—this can serve to educate the client. Consider the following as a script that is informative, educational, and yet doesn't reinforce anxiety:

Therapist: Henry, I'm sorry that you are still struggling with anxiety about your heart. The cardiologist's tests are clear that there is nothing wrong with your heart. You are having panic attacks. Panic attacks never cause a heart attack. I know that it is very difficult for you to stop worrying about your heart and it makes sense that you want to reassure yourself and fight this. Unfortunately, the things that you are doing to fight your anxiety are only making you feel worse. They may be helpful in the short term, but they actually fuel your anxiety in the long run. For example, how many times do you think you've checked your heart since you've been worried about this?

Henry:	Probably thousands.
Therapist:	What's the longest that checking your heart rate has helped?
Henry:	Truthfully, maybe an hour or two, but usually only a few seconds unless I'm really distracted.
Therapist:	So would you agree that this hasn't been very effective in reducing your anxiety?
Henry:	Right!
Therapist:	Getting reassurance from me, your wife, your parents, and even your doctor is the same, even though you don't do it as often. Now that I've told you my perspective, I won't repeat what I've said today or in future sessions, because I think it's more likely to feed your anxiety than to help it. Does this make sense?
Henry:	I see your point.
Therapist:	Are there any other things you do repetitively to try to manage your anxiety? Things that you feel compelled to do that help temporarily?
Henry:	I don't think so.
Therapist:	I expect that if you stop checking your heart rate and stop seeking reassurance from others you will feel more anxious in the short term. But my research and experience leaves me confident that you will feel much better than you do now in a few days. I'm wondering whether you'd be willing to do an experiment and try it just until our next appointment and see what happens?

If you, or your clients, are having problems grasping how this difficult concept of negative reinforcement works, *The Little Shop of Horrors* provides a great analogy. It is probably best known as a film, although it was first a book and then a musical play. It's not necessary to be familiar with the story to understand its relevance to negative reinforcement, but it may help. In *The Little Shop of Horrors*, a character by the name of Seymour purchases a small Venus fly trap, which he names "Audrey Jr." The plant starts off meekly and relatively infrequently asking Seymour to "feed me." After Seymour feeds the plant, it is quiet, and Seymour is relieved to have some peace. However, the plant grows and soon becomes hungry again, only to beg a little louder and a little more persistently. Each time Seymour feeds Audrey Jr., that temporarily quiets it, only to wind up making it grow larger, louder, and more persistent in its begging to be fed. Eventually, the once-small plant becomes so large and so out of control that it is insatiable and tries to eat people.

In this story, Seymour is negatively reinforced. The plant's begging is uncomfortable for him. When Seymour feeds the plant, he temporarily removes that discomfort. The fact that something is being removed makes it *negative* in operant conditioning. When we observe Seymour feed it again and again, we see that the behavior has increased, or in terms of operant conditioning, it has been *reinforced*. And we see that the begging is reinforced as it becomes worse. When it comes to GAD, this cycle occurs most frequently in hypochondriasis and perfectionism. We often see severe cycles of negative reinforcement in clients suffering from panic disorder, agoraphobia, OCD, and specific phobias. The plant is akin to the anxiety disorder, while feeding it is analogous to reassurance, avoidance, checking, and escape. Begging is analogous to anxiety. In order to stop the begging, Seymour would need to starve the plant by refraining from feeding it. While this would certainly lead to more persistence on the part of the plant in the short term, in the long run it would weaken the plant, causing the begging to cease eventually.

There are several other ways in which clients negatively reinforce anxiety. It is useful to assess for these habits early in therapy. If your client is engaging in negatively-reinforcing behaviors and these are left untreated, therapy will not be as effective. In fact, if at any time the coping strategies presented in this book are of little or no use, it might be that your client is engaging in negatively-reinforcing behaviors that are preventing the treatment from being effective. Therefore, it is helpful to identify and stop these behaviors first, before utilizing other treatment strategies. Some of these negatively-reinforcing behaviors are observable, but most of them are not. It may be obvious if your client is checking in the session or seeking reassurance from you. However, many of the negatively-reinforcing behaviors in which they might engage will not be observable. Examples include carrying Xanax in their purse or pocket, compulsive praying, and searching the internet at home. The following questions are useful for assessing the crutches clients may be using:

- What have you tried to do to reduce your anxiety?
- Is there anything you feel like you have to do when you are anxious?
- Do you find yourself ping-ponging or see-sawing between negative thoughts and reassuring thoughts in your mind?
- What do you avoid doing because of your anxiety?
- What makes you feel safer?

In addition to these questions, use the rest of your assessment to specifically guide questions to assess for negative reinforcement. So, for instance, if your client shares that they go to church regularly, ask whether their prayer habits have changed, because compulsive prayer is not uncommon in GAD, as well as in panic disorder and OCD. When used excessively to reduce anxiety, prayer is negatively reinforced and increases anxiety in the long run much like reassurance. Prayer and reassurance are both verbal recitations that can be performed in one's mind or aloud with the intention of reducing anxiety. Prayer introduces an additional challenge, because it's not ethical, or desirable, to interfere with our clients' religious values. However, in my experience, it is relatively easy to help a client reduce, or omit, the negative reinforcement involved in excessive prayer while still respecting their religious values.

When a religious client prays excessively, help them to understand the rationale of negative reinforcement and how prayer negatively reinforces their anxiety. Assess for what their prayer habits were like before they started having problematic anxiety and attempt to help them go back to those habits. Thus far, all my religious clients have been fine with this, even a couple of pastors.

What we tell our clients when we attempt to make them feel better can be cognitive therapy, reassurance, or education. Both cognitive therapy and education are sometimes helpful, but if you find yourself feeling a need to repeat yourself that should help, you are probably negatively reinforcing their anxiety, particularly if you notice that it helps temporarily. If your client doesn't believe it the first time, be careful about repeating it.

Similarly, there is also a fine line between cognitive therapy and reassurance. If a positive statement such as, "It's useless for me to worry about an unlikely event," works persistently for the client, it's cognitive therapy. If the positive statement is soon doubted and the client goes back to fearful thoughts and ping-ponging between the positive statement and the fearful thoughts, then it is reassurance and negatively reinforcing.

It's more difficult to control thoughts than behaviors. If your client is frequently reassuring themselves, ping-ponging between worries and neutralizing thoughts, it may be helpful to have them verbally face their fears. For instance, if Henry thought, "What if there is something wrong with my heart? Two doctors have assured me that my heart is fine. But what if they were wrong? They weren't wrong, I'm fine," and so forth, you could ask him to say these sentences aloud repeatedly: "What if there is something wrong with my heart? I'm afraid that the doctors missed something." By saying the feared thought repeatedly, the client stops negatively reinforcing the anxiety and eventually the anxiety is reduced or eliminated. In addition, you could say these fears aloud and ask the client to write them down. Consider doing the least threatening option first. Repeat until the anxiety has reduced significantly or is low.

There are also several free apps for audio loops such that the client can record two or three sentences that repeat for a specified time period or number of repetitions. Sometimes clients enjoy an immediate reduction in anxiety because the sentences sound ridiculous when you or the client say them aloud. Use other strategies if the client has poor insight—that is, if they are convinced that their negative thought is true. Most clients recognize at some level that their worries aren't true.

SUBSTANCES THAT NEGATIVELY REINFORCE AND POSITIVELY REINFORCE ANXIETY

There are many ways that people commonly negatively reinforce their anxiety. One of the most common is the use of medication. Benzodiazepines, such as alprazolam (Xanax), lorazepam (Ativan), and clonazepam (Klonopin), are often very effective at reducing anxiety in the short term while strengthening the fear in the long term. In addition, these medications often make clients feel good, thereby positively reinforcing taking the medication as well. Furthermore, nothing is learned about managing anxiety. When the medication wears off, clients' anxiety usually returns, and they usually feel the need to take more, often in increasingly higher doses.

If you believe that it's wrong to encourage clients to drink alcohol to manage anxiety, the same principles apply to benzodiazepines. These medications are worse than alcohol because clients who would never drink alcohol at work or in the morning freely use these medications at all times and in all situations. Furthermore, because their physician, or similar health care professional, prescribed them, they are even more likely to use them than alcohol. Xanax negatively reinforces anxiety the most because it is the quickest acting and has the shortest half-life. Klonopin reinforces anxiety the least, especially when taken as a scheduled dose. It may be indicated to ask your client's prescriber to switch them to Klonopin or Xanax XR before titrating, while the client is learning the strategies in their workbook. Whether clients are self-medicating with alcohol, illicit drugs, or prescribed medication, referral to a substance abuse specialist may be indicated either before treatment for anxiety or concurrently. For more information about the weaning process, there is a wonderful set of books called *Stopping Anxiety Medication*. One is a therapist manual (Otto & Pollack, 2009b) and the other is a client workbook (Otto & Pollack, 2009a).

The "P" Sheet and Preferred Ways to Think Instead of Worrying

The "P" Sheet is something that you can use in your practice to remind you to use these strategies with clients. You may also start a partial "P" Sheet after you have taught a client three or four of these strategies and add a row to the sheet after you have taught them a new one. Another idea is for you to use this list, and add some of your own strategies that don't fit into the "Ps," to include in each client's file to keep track of which strategies you have taught them.

Ask your client to bring in their "P" Sheet each week for you to look over. This serves a dual purpose. Self-monitoring in and of itself improves compliance. If your client knows that you will be looking at their work during their next appointment, not only will they be more likely to complete the sheet, but they will also be more likely to engage in the strategies more often. That is, the first purpose of the "P" Sheet is to increase compliance.

The second reason is to help provide suggestions in the future. After listening to what went well in the week and what didn't go well, you can look at which strategies were used and make suggestions. For instance, if your client relays a time that their anxiety got out of control and they didn't check "Prevent," you can help them to increase or change their reminders for early cue detection. Or, if they got depressed and you see that they didn't check off gratefulness or B^{3}s very often, you could suggest that they get back into those habits and even brainstorm B^{3}s with them. You could also ask the client to recite in the session things for which they are grateful.

Finally, if they are using number estimates and you see that they had a particularly high number for estimates of prayer, it may have become an unhealthy compulsion. It's not unusual for a religion to require four to six instances of prayer in the day. Scheduled prayer, evening prayers, and prayers at meals are often very healthy and helpful. However, when you see double-digit estimates, it's likely that clients are using prayer as a crutch. See Therapist Chapter 15, page 160, for advice on how to manage excessive, compulsive prayer habits.

Getting Motivated to Manage Depression

Low motivation is a common symptom of depression. However, unless the depression is severe, clients usually feel better once they get out of the house to socialize or exercise or once they get started on responsibilities they have been avoiding. If possible, help clients identify recent times when they were on the fence about socializing or when they had sex when they weren't sure if they had the energy. Then ask them whether they were mostly glad they did it or mostly sorry they did it. While some clients say that they were sorry because they didn't enjoy it or that they were neither sorry nor happy, usually people say that they enjoyed it more than they thought they would. Others say they are glad that they engaged in the activity because they felt it was better than staying home again (in the case of socializing) or missing an opportunity for closeness with their partner (in the case of sex). Encourage clients to remember this the next time they aren't sure whether they want to go out, have people over, engage in a hobby, or have sex.

Similarly, ask them how many times they didn't want to exercise or complete a small task, but did it anyway. If they had a positive response, encourage them to remember that, once they found a way to motivate themselves, they usually were glad they did it and felt better. Hopefully this will be helpful to motivate them in the future.

When clients are in doubt about whether they were happy they engaged in an activity they had been on the fence about, encourage them to do behavioral experiments. Below is a script with a client who thinks they should exercise, but keeps avoiding it.

> Therapist: Next time you are thinking that you should exercise, remind yourself of why you want to exercise. What are those reasons?
> Client: I feel better when I'm done. I sleep better too.
> Therapist: I know it's very difficult for you to get motivated, but I'm wondering whether you could find the energy to exercise for just 15 minutes. Would you be willing to do an experiment and see what happens if you commit to a 15-minute walk?
> Client: I can try that.
> Therapist: Give yourself permission to stop or keep going after 15 minutes. Whether you continue to exercise or stop at that point, ask yourself whether you were glad you did it. Fill out this five-point scale [as shown on p. 85 of the client workbook].

You could use a similar script with cleaning the house, cooking, running errands, getting back into a hobby, or any number of things. However, because exercise helps depression too, helping to motivate clients to exercise is often key.

If clients aren't going to exercise and aren't willing to socialize or engage in activities that used to bring them pleasure, medication may be indicated. Likewise, medication may be indicated if clients do engage in these activities and find that they aren't enjoyable, especially if the other measures in this workbook aren't helpful in managing their depression. For clients who are resistant, sometimes urging them to consider medication is what motivates them to start using the principles in this book. Also see the information on working with treatment-resistant clients in Therapist Chapter 24, as well as the second portion of Therapist Chapter 22, on procrastination.

Liberate Yourself:
Say "No"

Traditionally, you may think of clients who put others ahead of themselves as being co-dependent. However, this term is associated with substance dependency and substance abuse. Many clients who are self-sacrificing take care of people who have no problems with substances. The person receiving help might just be happy to have help with a medical condition, an Axis I disorder, or old age. Individuals with Axis II disorders, especially narcissistic personality disorder and dependent personality disorder, seek out these individuals and take advantage of them. These clients may also take on too much responsibility at work, may volunteer too much, or may even help strangers too much.

Often these clients choose helping professions, such as being a nurse, a teacher, a caregiver, or (yes, you guessed it) a psychotherapist. If you think your life is out of balance because you put others' needs ahead of your own time after time, you may want to use the workbook portion for this habit before you start helping others with it.

People who help people when it's not their responsibility, or in a way that goes beyond the call of duty, make the world a better place. It's great that we have good samaritans and volunteers. It's wonderful that we have friends who help us. Likewise, it's important to honor these traits in ourselves and in our clients. But a healthy balance is the key! This means helping others, but also helping ourselves and meeting our own needs.

The first step to achieve this balance is to help clients determine the difference between the nice and helpful things they *want* to do and the things that they do out of guilt or fear. Sometimes knowing the difference is tricky, especially when these acts of kindness are hybrids of wanting to help and feeling obliged to help. One of the main roles of the therapist is to help clients sort out what is healthy for them to do and what they are unhealthily doing for others out of duty, fear, or guilt.

When clients simply are not certain, there are a few possibilities to consider:

- Find a compromise between what they are doing now and not doing it at all.
- See whether the client is willing to try to not do it and see how it feels.
- Similarly, if your client can't decide how much they *want* to do something and how much of their desire is driven by guilt and/or fear, encourage them to say "no." This can help them to know how they really feel about it. Once they know, they can choose a compromise or agree to the request.
- Get the client very relaxed and have them visualize saying "no," imagining not doing the thing they've been asked to, and seeing how it feels. Then imagine doing it and seeing how it feels.
- Put the shoe on the other foot. That is, ask them to put a friend in the role and imagine the friend not doing it. How would the client view the friend for saying "no"? Is their judgment fair?

Because the client is used to saying "yes" and may not have good assertiveness skills to say "no," teaching assertiveness skills may be necessary. Role-plays are particularly helpful because you can model appropriate assertive behaviors while the client gets practice creating healthier boundaries. It's best to start by having the client play the person to whom they want to say "no" to or with whom they intend to initiate a compromise. By experiencing what the person is like you can develop more empathy and be a better model for assertive behavior. Then, when you switch roles and have your client play themselves, they will be better prepared to be assertive in the role-play and, thereby, in real life. Often, I will be very persistent to help the client face the discomfort; if the role-play is more difficult, the client will be prepared if their attempts to create a boundary are met with resistance. Also, it increases the likelihood that their actual situation will be easier, thereby rewarding their assertive efforts.

People who are not accustomed to being assertive may not make appropriate eye contact, may speak too softly, and may have passive posture. Be prepared to encourage clients to make eye contact, speak confidently, and stand or sit tall. Consider recommending a book on assertiveness, particularly if you aren't good at it yourself. One that is specific to the issue at hand is *When I Say No, I Feel Guilty* (Smith, 1985). *The Assertive Option* (Jakubowski & Lange, 1978) is dated in some vignettes, but the principles are strong and clear and the authors are excellent at explaining the differences between assertive, aggressive, and passive behaviors, as well as giving several examples.

Most people who put others' needs ahead of their own have a really difficult time asking for help when they could use a hand. Particularly if they have friends, colleagues, and relatives whom they have helped, or if there is someone it just makes sense to ask (e.g., a retired neighbor could take them to drop off their car for its service), help the client role-play asking for help.

Keep in mind that negative reinforcement plays a role for self-sacrificing people. While there may be some negative reinforcement of fear, there is mostly negative reinforcement of guilt. While clients are sometimes positively reinforced with praise, expressions of appreciation, and a sense of feeling good about doing kind things, they may also be self-sacrificing to avoid the feeling of guilt. If they are helpful, they won't feel guilty; if they say "no," they might feel guilty. To avoid feeling guilty, they put others' needs ahead of their own. Often the habit of helping is so automatic that the client isn't even aware of whether guilt and fear are involved. Fortunately, you can also help them label the feeling of guilt as "helpful" or "not helpful."

Fortunately, once the client creates healthy boundaries, the feeling of guilt is often less than the individual expects. Furthermore, a feeling of empowerment typically prevails. Nonetheless, use cognitive therapy to reduce guilty feelings and encourage your client to get comfortable with the discomfort while recognizing that the feelings of guilt, while understandable due to negative reinforcement, are not to be trusted.

Encourage your client to use the giving receiving & saying no monitoring form provided in the workbook (p. 93). Given that self-sacrificing clients like to please people, knowing that they will be showing you their monitoring form is likely to increase their compliance. Of course, we want our clients to change these behaviors for themselves rather than to please you. But, in the end, it's better for them to learn to reduce their self-sacrificing behaviors even if part of why they are doing it is to please you. If you sense that it is a problem, processing this in the session can be helpful and they can even include you on their self-monitoring form.

One final consideration: If the situation at hand is too uncomfortable and too challenging, your client is more likely to fail. Consider using easier situations first, even if they aren't as important. Angry, aggressive, entitled people will be more difficult targets and the risk for client failure to stand up for their rights is increased. Help them to begin by choosing someone who is more likely to respect their assertiveness.

Catastrophizing? Accepting Uncertainty

A major role for therapists treating worry about catastrophizing is helping clients to internalize the fact that most of the major tragedies in life cannot be prevented. Even if we were to choose a very reclusive, unfulfilling life to reduce the likelihood, catastrophes can happen at home. While it may make sense to get an alarm system in unsafe areas, an alarm system in safe areas may reinforce the idea that the potential for danger is much higher than it is. Likewise, other measures to improve safety, or to attempt to improve safety, may be serving to negatively reinforce anxiety. These include over-checking and avoidance behaviors. Refer to Therapist Chapter 15 for information on assessing and treating these problematic behaviors.

Helping your clients to accept uncertainty is key. Their worries are not useful. The goal is to help them recognize that their worries will not prevent bad things from happening and that their worried habits only cause anxiety, frustration, and depression. If a client does believe that their worry decreases the likelihood of things happening or prevents them from happening, refer to the next chapter, which addresses these superstitious beliefs and behaviors.

Most clients agree that, if the bad thing does happen, they will not be glad that they worried about it. However, some clients do believe that they will be glad that they worried about a tragic event because they believe it will create a buffer. That is, they think that if they worry about something, such as the sudden and tragic death of their spouse, it won't be quite as difficult if it happens. There certainly is the possibility that worry does create a buffer; however, in the second half of the next chapter, there are specific strategies to manage this reason for worry.

When clients do *not* believe that worry will act as a buffer if a tragic event occurs, use the labels "useful" and "useless" or similar (e.g., "helpful" and "not helpful"). Regardless of whether they believe in worry as a buffer, it can be particularly helpful to have clients label their thoughts as "fact" or "fiction." Point out, too, that even when bad things happen, they don't ever turn out exactly as we had feared, so such worries are always "fiction." If the client is stuck on the idea that anything is possible and the worst-case scenario could be true, you could have them label a worry "closer to fiction" or even adjust their thinking about the labels so that "fiction" means "probably fiction." Listen to how your client describes their exaggerated fears and consider using their labels. For instance, one of my clients described his negative thinking in exaggerating the likelihood of a tragic event as "bullshit." I recommended that he use the labels "fact" and "bullshit" after that, and it was particularly useful.

Encourage your client to use the "Worry Outcome Diary" in Chapter 19. Many clients resist using this, but it is very effective when they do use it. In the event of poor adherence to it, you can encourage clients to make the log much simpler. For example, they could simply record two or three words for the worry along with a numbered outcome rating (e.g., "Cameron's late; 1") on an electronic device, on a small notepad or piece of paper, or in the back of their paper calendar. Whether a client is doing the full or short version of this monitoring, it is significantly more useful if they write the worry down while they are worrying rather than after the event has transpired. Be sure to assess for this and encourage tweaking if needed. This worksheet is particularly useful for catastrophizing because we usually learn the reality within days, often even minutes, after the worry begins. However, it is useful for all worries in which the client will learn the outcome soon. Therefore, don't limit the use of this monitoring form to catastrophizing.

International news significantly contributes to clients' fears of tragedies. It's not at all natural for us to learn of so much trauma in the world. Also, modern transportation and increasingly-deadly weapons put us at much greater actual risk for tragic accidents and mass shootings than our ancestors. If we watch or read the news, we are subjected to painful stories, sometimes daily. On the one hand, avoiding the news can reduce exposure to these tragic events. On the other hand, sometimes avoidance behaviors can make it more painful when we are made aware of these situations by others. In addition, avoiding the news can lead to being uninformed in useful areas of life.

One thing about watching the news is clear. There is certainly a point at which people become too connected to the news, particularly after learning of a specific tragedy, such that limiting exposure is indicated. If too much news is a problem, it may be helpful to avoid it completely at first. Then you can suggest clients gradually introduce limited exposure to news. Encourage your client to experiment with limiting their exposure (e.g., 30 minutes per day of specific news coverage) or temporarily stop watching and reading the news.

It also may be helpful to connect with your clients in a heartfelt way about their desire to control tragedy. The following is an example of what you might say.

> *With all the horrible tragedies we see in the news today, it's painful to think of a similar tragedy affecting your family. Especially given that you have so many wonderful things in your life with your young family, you have more to lose than ever. This is a great thing about your life! So it's completely understandable that you would want to have control over something horrible happening. I know you really wish you could prevent bad things from happening to you and your family. In fact, I wonder whether your worry is a way to feel as if you do have control over the awful things that you see happening to others in the world? [Client responds; perhaps a discussion ensues.] Unfortunately, the things that you worry about are largely outside your control. In fact, I wonder whether the very things you are doing to try to control these things make your life out of control? [Perhaps an additional query about how their worry is negatively impacting their life.]*

> *The families you see stricken by tragedy, such as [name the most recent thing the client has seen or heard about, if applicable], would not have prevented tragedy from happening if they had worried more. And it's very important to recognize that the news doesn't cover the billions of people who get through life without significant tragedy. In fact, how many people do you know who are senior citizens who have never suffered a tragic event? Can you imagine being in your seventies or eighties with your husband/wife, kids, and grandkids, looking back on all the time and energy you spent wasted on worrying about things that never happened? And, in the unlikely event that a tragedy occurs, don't you want to enjoy your life before it happens?*

There are some tragedies that could have been controlled. Even in these rare cases, though, the person at fault is usually someone who was very careless and very different from the client. In any event, in some cases, it may be helpful for the client to exercise "due diligence." Point out how the client is already doing what is necessary to minimize, or even prevent, the possibility of the tragic event occurring, or how the client is different from the people involved in a rare tragedy that could have been prevented (e.g., would never leave their child unattended in a car or leave a candle burning after going to bed).

If the client doesn't respond to the suggestions in this chapter, the following chapter may be helpful if they are superstitious or believe that worry can serve as a buffer if something tragic does occur. Otherwise, assess for the possibility that the client needs to process a traumatic event from earlier in life that may be driving this fear. Consider a referral if you do not specialize in the treatment of trauma, particularly if the client is not making progress.

Therapist 20 Chapter

Superstitious? What's the Evidence?

The therapist's role is to help clients see that they have no evidence that their worry has a protective effect. The only thoughts that affect outcomes are those aimed at planning and problem-solving. Once the client has read Chapter 20 and used the accompanying worksheet, they should start to question the utility of their worries and feel the futility of them more. It is recommended that you read the Socratic questioning in Chapter 20, which is designed to start to break down clients' faulty belief systems and behaviors about superstition. Process this further with a discussion about the lack of evidence and the desire to control the uncontrollable. Perhaps you can also help the client to see how their attempts to control their life do the opposite. Discuss how their life is made more out of control by these attempts to assert control, sharing some of the symptoms they reported to you at intake or during the course of therapy.

Once you believe you and your client have done what you can to break down their faulty beliefs, ask your client whether they would be willing to do a behavioral experiment. Encourage them to revisit the strategies to reduce worry for a specific time period or for an event (see Chapter 6) and see whether the things they were fearful of come to fruition. For instance, "Would you be willing to use strategies to reduce your worry until our next session and see what happens?" Or, "Next time you are worried about one of your children driving home from college, would you be willing to do your best to use strategies to manage worry and see whether they get home alright?"

Some clients may engage in superstitious behaviors. Such behaviors are more often seen in OCD than in GAD or depression. They are negatively reinforced in two ways. First, the client feels less anxious after they engage in the behaviors. Second, they may inappropriately believe that because the feared event didn't occur, their compulsion was responsible. Again, approach this Socratically: "What's the likelihood that, had you not knocked on wood three times, the same result would have occurred?" And, again, ask whether the client would be willing to do an experiment: "Next time you feel the desire to knock on wood, would you be willing to resist that urge and see what happens?"

If your client believes that worry about a tragedy will make it less painful if one happens, ask the client if they know how much they would need to worry for it to be a buffer. Most have no idea, but it gets them to thinking about the fact that they probably don't need to worry as much as they do to buffer it. The idea here is to have them engage in controlled worry to buffer the fear and worry much less.

I believe the best way to do this is to have them postpone their worries to specific worry periods, as done in Therapist Chapter 6. Depending upon the severity or their schedule, ask them to worry at least four specific times per week, daily, or on week days for a specific amount of time from 15 to 30 minutes. Once they have finished that worry period, each time they begin to worry, they can postpone their worry to the following worry period and gently move their mind to a coping strategy such as mindfulness. This way, they are accomplishing two things. First, they are managing the worry, instead of the worry controlling them. Second, they are giving their concerns a form of due diligence to have the buffer they want. If this is enough to manage the worry in between worry sessions and the client feels it will create the buffer they desire, reduce the number of sessions, the amount of time, or both.

If the client finds that they still worry situationally, (e.g. when loved ones are traveling) ask them to set a timer for three minutes and worry intently, without distractions, for three minutes. When that three minutes is up, have them postpone the worry to when they hear from the person they are worried about, to when they learn of other news, or to the next worry session. For instance, their spouse is flying back from a business trip. Once they start to worry about it, have them set a timer and worry about it for three minutes. After that, have them postpone the worry to the time they hear from their spouse. Provide strategies to help the client resist urges to call or text the spouse or even watch the news to see whether some tragedy may have occurred.

Hypochondriasis

Treating hypochondriasis can be particularly challenging. Most of these clients overuse the health care system, seeing doctors for every little concern. Less commonly, clients may do the opposite: Because they are afraid of getting bad news, they avoid seeing doctors unless their symptoms are unbearable. There is rarely a healthy medium.

There is a joke that highlights some of the difficulties in managing these clients. The doctor says to their patient, "I have good news and bad news. The good news is you aren't a hypochondriac." The point is that clients who suffer from hypochondriasis aren't immune to medical problems. We can never assume that the client doesn't have a serious illness. Similarly, if a client certainly has panic attacks, that doesn't mean that there isn't a medical condition involved. Also, some may have a medical condition, but still have hypochondriasis about benign symptoms whether they are related to that medical condition or not. Finally, in some cases, a relatively benign diagnosis is given to a client, but the client believes it is very serious or the wrong diagnosis. For instance, a client might have been diagnosed with mitral valve prolapse (a relatively benign condition) and also be convinced that they have a life-threatening arrhythmia or heart defect.

Always assess how much your client is using the internet to explore their symptoms or excessively searching for information on a confirmed diagnosis. Compulsively searching the internet is one of the most common and problematic symptoms of hypochondriasis. Therefore, one of the first things I do is suggest that clients do an experiment. "Would you be willing to stay off the internet just until our next session?" If possible, get them to agree to avoid both social media and news media and not just avoid medical sites. This is because there are often disease-related topics on sites other than medically-related sites. Rule out whether they are subscribers to any medical sites, and if they are, recommend that they unsubscribe.

Clients are often surprised by how much better they feel after resisting the urge to get on these sites. Often clients know they will benefit from this, and many have had a family member or friend suggest that they stop or limit their searching. Having a professional tell them to get off the internet is often the motivation they need to stop. When clients resist, try to get them to limit their use to an agreed-upon amount of time (less than 20 minutes per day) and to stick to a cut-off time at night (90 minutes prior to their desired bedtime). Also encourage them to limit their sources to one or two respected sites (such as WebMD.com or MayoClinic.org, or, if they have a verified medical problem, the site of a respected organization that is relevant to their condition, such as the American Heart Association: Heart.org).

Sometimes people with hypochondriasis can be diagnosed with OCD or panic disorder. You will most commonly see OCD among people who are fearful of contracting infectious diseases. Often, it's the most recent outbreak that people fear the most. In 2014 to 2015, Ebola was particularly feared. Back in the 1980s, OCD about contracting AIDS/HIV was particularly common. A distinguishing feature of OCD is that clients obsess about having the disease even when they haven't engaged in any risky behaviors and after testing has proven they are healthy. For instance, a clean (non-drug using) and straight man who has been faithful to his wife might fear that he has contracted the HIV virus from using a public restroom, even after testing negative for the virus. For OCD, use the strategies in Therapist Chapter 15, on crutches. For more information on treating OCD, try *Brain Based Therapy for OCD: A Workbook for Clinicians and Clients* (Arden, 2014) or *Freedom from Obsessive Compulsive Disorder: A Personalized Recovery Program for Living with Uncertainty* (Grayson, 2014).

Panic attacks with hypochondriasis typically revolve around either cardiac symptoms or brain-related symptoms, such as feeling derealized, dizzy, lightheaded, or faint. If clients worry their way into a panicked state, this workbook may be sufficient. However, if they fear the symptoms or are having out-of-the-blue panic, I'd suggest *Panic Attacks Workbook: A Guided Program for Beating the Panic Trick* (Carbonell, 2014) for clients or *Resistant Anxiety, Worry, & Panic: 86 Practical Treatment Strategies for Clinicians* (Abel, 2014) for therapists. Lower levels of anxiety can cause uncomfortable physiological symptoms and contribute to medical problems, sometimes a self-fulfilling prophecy (see p. 106 of the Client Workbook).For more information on treating hypochondriasis see *Hypochondriasis and Health Anxiety* (Abramowitz & Braddock, 2010).

In some cases, it is advised to have a conversation with the client's physician about stopping unnecessary tests and establishing guidelines for when the client should and shouldn't call for an appointment. Doctors who are desperately trying to finally put the client's mind at ease often inadvertently negatively reinforce the fear by seeing their patient repeatedly and running several tests, sometimes at the client's urging. Physicians want to treat medical problems, so they are usually relieved to get your help with managing these problematic clients.

Procrastination

There are two general types of procrastinators: those who are successful at procrastinating and those who run out of time, get bad grades, do poorly at work, and suffer additional negative consequences. The reality is that research indicates that people who procrastinate, but eventually end up getting things accomplished, fare better than pre-crastinators (those who get things done right away). While pre-crastinators do alright, people who procrastinate but complete their goal are usually more creative and generally more successful (Subotnik, Steiner, & Chakraborty, 1999). For these clients, the biggest concerns are worrying about getting started and being shamed by others who are uncomfortable with their procrastinating. Both can fuel anxiety and guilt about procrastinating.

When clients successfully procrastinate pressure themselves, either because they think they should get started or because they are getting heat from others to get in gear, encourage them to accept their procrastination. Use cognitive therapy to help them embrace their habit. Below is a list of possible B^3s about their procrastination:

- They are more creative when the heat is on.
- Their concentration is better.
- They stay on target. That is, they don't get distracted by the phone, the internet, or doing less important things that tend to pull them away when they try to start early.
- The worst thing that has happened is that they've lost sleep or got grief from "pre-crastinators." Or maybe they occasionally miss out on something fun.
- They usually, if not always, do well: They get good grades or succeed at work.
- They spend less total time to accomplish their goal.
- The benefits of procrastination outweigh the costs.
- Research supports that a habit of procrastination is more often an advantage than a disadvantage.

To manage worry associated with meeting a deadline, have the client use the postponing technique. For more detail on how this applies to procrastination, see Chapter 22, which covers planned procrastination. The steps are outlined on page 110.

An important role for you as a therapist is to help your client's loved ones, and occasionally co-workers, accept your client's procrastination. A family session may be indicated, particularly if your client is living with a parent who is putting pressure them. Essentially, you will cover the list above as it applies to your client. Alternatively, help your client to be assertive with others who put pressure on them to start earlier. Whether you have a discussion with family members in the session or prep your client to be assertive, stating the fact that procrastination is not always a bad thing is a good place to start. Of course, it's useful to include education about the facts about moderate procrastination being an advantage over pre-crastination. If family members are still skeptical, suggest that they watch a TED Talk by Adam Grant titled "The Surprising Habits of Original Thinkers" (2016), in which Grant explains the benefits of procrastination.

There are at least three reasons that procrastination is better for some people. One is that ideas may be "marinating" in the brain while they are procrastinating. Second, when the pressure is on, people might be more creative than usual. This is consistent with the Yerkes–Dodson law (1908), in which a moderate amount of arousal yields the greatest productivity (for more on this law, see p.117). Third, when people procrastinate, once they start working, they are much less likely to give in to external distractions such as the phone, TV, and searching the internet. Similarly, they are also more likely to be focused and less likely to daydream. The last two points are particularly true of people with ADHD, who may not be able to focus unless the heat is on. The bottom line with procrastination: It's only a problem if it's a problem.

Parents may push back if the child tends to lose too much sleep. If this doesn't affect their physical or mental health, encourage the parent to accept it. However, if the child becomes very irritable or tends to get sick, some problem-solving measures to reduce this interference are suggested (e.g., insisting on a nap or solitary activity after school the next day). Also, some of the measures that are used for unsuccessful procrastinators can be integrated and a compromise can be reached.

For individuals who procrastinate too long, help them to break activities down into smaller pieces. This can be done in three ways:

1. Choose a specific amount of time to work on the activity (usually, 10 minutes to an hour).
2. Choose a small piece of the larger task.
3. Choose a small piece of the larger task with a goal of getting it completed at a specific time.

If clients are uncertain which of the above strategies would work best for them, encourage them to experiment. Keep in mind that different tasks may call for different strategies and varying amounts of time commitment. Also, clients may benefit from some guidance on dividing the larger task into subtasks. Furthermore, for huge tasks, such as a thesis or preparing a house for sale and moving, dividing the work into tertiary tasks may be helpful. This level of detail may be helpful for some clients and is not outlined in the client workbook.

I will use myself as an example. I procrastinated about everything in high school and as an undergrad. I knew that I couldn't do that with my dissertation. To get motivated, I divided it into several small, doable tasks. I started by looking at big chunks—for instance, "write the introduction." This involved doing a literature review, for which I needed to find 20 articles, read those and take notes and highlight them, summarize them into a draft, get feedback from my dissertation chair, and eventually finish the introduction. I decided when I'd like to finish the introduction, as well as all of the other major tasks, and wrote these dates in my planner. I wrote in these goals over the few months up to the proposal meeting.

Once the proposal was accepted, I broke the rest of the work into a few major tasks. Then I broke the first major task into subtasks that could be accomplished in about a week and wrote them in my planner. Then, at the beginning of each week, I divided the weekly goal into six daily tasks. I wrote each successive task on Monday through Saturday of my planner. This method allowed me an extra day if I had underestimated the amount of time the tasks would take or if I had an unusually busy week. It also allowed a day to break from my dissertation if the tasks went well. I completed my dissertation before my internship—a feat seldom accomplished. Consider how you can apply a similar strategy to people who are undertaking large goals they have been procrastinating about.

In addition, I made a commitment to my dissertation chair to have each of the milestones accomplished. It helps to have accountability to keep clients on track, especially with large projects. Whether the client is completing a dissertation, cleaning out their basement, or preparing a house for sale, encourage them to make a commitment to you, as well as friends and relatives who support them in accomplishing their feats. Encourage clients to check in with their support on at least a weekly basis. Ideally, they can find someone else who is trying to accomplish a similar goal and they can support one another.

Perfectionism

Perfectionism is often difficult to treat. Typically, clients have been positively reinforced for their perfectionism and often have been punished for making mistakes. They are also usually negatively reinforced for their behavior. Whether it's the aching feeling that it isn't quite right going away once they feel it is perfect, whether it's constantly being busy to avoid the guilt associated with not being productive, or whether they *feel* as though they escaped feared consequences, negative reinforcement can make it very difficult for a person to stop perfectionism.

Unfortunately, the habit is often so engrained that it isn't changeable unless the client's unbalanced and stressed life has led to significant suffering. The more the client has suffered from their unrealistic standards and the more stable they feel in their career and relationships, the more likely they are to find the motivation to loosen their standards.

Encourage your client to "get comfortable with being uncomfortable" regarding perfectionistic behaviors that the client knows to be unrealistic and excessive, but still feels uncomfortable about when loosening those standards. Instead of them negatively reinforcing their fears by being perfect to avoid discomfort, the goal is to feel the discomfort. Encourage them to: stop at "very good" or "good enough," do something fun when their to-do list is long, take a weekly date night regardless of other responsibilities, or allow a minor mistake to go uncorrected. With time, the discomfort will lessen and clients will begin to enjoy being more balanced.

Perfectionism often begins when a child has little control over their environment. If they were bullied at school or abused at home, academic work, looking perfect, or managing a restrictive diet could have been a way to have control and often the only way they were able to get validation and positive reinforcement. What was adaptive in childhood and in teenage years often is maladaptive later. Accessing emotion (as discussed in Chapter 11) may be indicated, particularly if the client has difficulty letting go of their perfectionistic standards.

For clients who are success-oriented, encourage them to aim for creating a successful life, rather than being a success. A good way to start with this is Socratically:

> *On your deathbed, do you think you are more likely to regret that you didn't work harder and be more perfect or do you think you'll be more likely to regret that you didn't pursue your passions, enjoy time with loved ones, and have more fun?*

This probably won't be helpful with most teens and twenty-somethings, but often this is a great motivator for middle-aged clients who are feeling more and more that their perfectionism is making their lives much less perfect. I recommend sharing the information collected by a hospice worker who recorded many of her dying patients' regrets on their deathbed (Ware, 2012). "I wish I hadn't worked so hard" was only number two. Number one basically fit into "I wish I'd had the courage to live a life true to myself, not the life others expected of me." To accentuate the effect, lean in and speak softly to clients: "Don't let these be your regrets later in life. You have time to change these habits."

If you would like an additional resource to help your clients, the book *When Perfect Isn't Good Enough: Strategies for Coping with Perfectionism* (Antony & Swinson, 2009) is empirically supported for its effectiveness.

All perfectionistic subjects in a study by Pleva and Wade (2007) used an earlier edition of Antony and Swinson's book. Half of the subjects were on their own and half had guidance from therapists. The "pure self-help" improved, but those who received therapists' guidance enjoyed significantly more improvement.

Resistant Clients

There are three types of resistant clients. The first is those who are on board. They listen and follow through with your suggestions in therapy. However, despite their greatest efforts and your greatest efforts, improvement is limited. The second type wants to be on board and is respectful, but follow-through is limited and they don't improve much. The third type is those who have a resistant personality. These are the clients who question you, look for reasons why your suggestions won't work, make excuses, and don't follow through. Of course, the implications for treating each of these clients differ significantly.

For those who are compliant and try CBT, rule out negatively-reinforcing behaviors. If clients are engaging in these behaviors, they may remain stuck, despite making great effort with the strategies in the workbook. Revisit the questions in Therapist Chapter 15 on page 160.

Also look for deeper issues and consider more traditional methods or experiential therapies, as outlined in Therapist Chapter 11, on healthy emotion. Consider this especially if the client has a history of trauma or avoids emotional processing, as evidenced by avoiding talking about sensitive topics, minimizing emotional topics, or exhibiting flat affect when talking about such topics (although flat affect can be an indication of depression). Look at social relationships too. We derive a great deal of our enjoyment from people, so clients who have a poor social support network are likely to be depressed. Furthermore, in one study, those who had problems with social relationships improved less with CBT for GAD than those who had a healthier social life (Borkovec, Newman, Pincus, & Lytle, 2002). Finally, in depressed clients, remember the importance of ruling out GAD or otherwise excessive worry and treat it.

For the compliant group of clients, as well as those who are respectful but just can't seem to follow through, consider whether hormones may be an issue. Imbalances in sex hormones, vitamin D, and thyroid hormones are all known to be associated with depression and anxiety.

Sex hormones can cause or contribute to depression, anxiety, insomnia, and irritability at any age. It is particularly important to rule out hormonal issues if the client has experienced a seemingly inexplicable increase of symptoms into middle age. We typically think of women as going through menopause and only men as needing testosterone, but men and women can both lose testosterone into middle age. Bio-identical hormones are recommended over synthetic ones, but both may be contraindicated for some individuals, especially those at high risk for breast cancer. Physician opinion on the use of hormones varies greatly, but the use of bio-identical hormone replacement therapy is becoming increasingly common.

Vitamin D deficits are more likely to cause depression, but can also contribute to anxiety. The "new normal" is that 21st-century people don't get enough sun as compared to our ancestors. The new normal is not healthy. Vitamin D is a hormone that can be low at any age and is particularly important the further north a client lives or if your client experiences a seasonal pattern such that their mood gets worse as the days get shorter.

When recommending a dosage of vitamin D supplements, most laboratories consider 20 ng/ml or 30 ng/ml to be in the normal range. However, physicians who are in the know recommend that patients have at least 50 ng/ml of vitamin D per day and some as much as 100 ng/ml.

On the one hand, pale clients who obviously avoid the sun may be at greater risk. On the other hand, darker skin requires more light to synthesize vitamin D, such that African Americans may need as much as 10 times as much sun to synthesize the same amount of vitamin D as a Caucasian. You might erroneously conclude that obese people will be at less risk due to having more skin to absorb sunlight, but they also do not absorb vitamin D from the sun as well. Those over 50 also do not absorb vitamin D as readily.

Finally, an imbalance in the thyroid can lead to depressive symptoms. Typically, low thyroid leads to depression, while high thyroid leads to anxiety. Low iron can lead to low energy and, thereby, low motivation and is particularly common in women. Women who exercise regularly are more likely to be low in iron. There are several other medical causes of anxiety and depression. A visit to a physician can be helpful. Keep in mind, though, that if hormones or other causes of depression or anxiety are present, including a sedentary lifestyle, medications such as selective serotonin re-uptake inhibitors (or SSRIs) may be treating the symptoms rather than the cause.

When people do not follow through, but have good intentions in the session, rule out ADHD and depression. Difficulty getting motivated is a common symptom of depression and may be the symptom that interferes the most with therapy. If a client cannot get motivated to follow through with your suggestions due to inertia, medication is indicated unless the client is more motivated to exercise. Exercise increases the stimulation of serotonin and norepinephrine, which help with both depression and anxiety. It also stimulates dopamine, which makes us happy.

Clients with ADHD often lack the concentration necessary to engage in many of the strategies or they forget what was discussed or forget to use them. When a lack of concentration is driven by boredom, doing more active forms of relaxation with more stimulation is more likely to be effective. Consider a mindfulness walk and more rapidly vary the focus with all of your relaxation patter. Encourage your client to take notes in the session if forgetfulness is an issue. In addition, brainstorm reminders for them to engage in their skills more regularly and have them set reminders on their smartphone while in the session. Similarly, hand them sticky notes so they are more likely to remember to do the strategy when they find the note in their purse or pocket. Also consider treating ADHD with a referral for medication or alternative methods such as neurobiofeedback.

Finally, for difficult clients, use the Socratic method. They are more likely to be engaged when they believe they are coming to their own conclusions and will keep more of an open mind than when being told what to do. Avoid getting into a power struggle. Rather, when they say that something won't work, ask them whether they are willing to do an experiment. If they say they already tried that, ask them for details and tweak. Here's an example:

Therapist: Do you exercise?

Client: No.

Therapist: Exercise can really help with both depression and anxiety. It's a natural antidepressant and anxiolytic.

Client: I already tried exercise and it didn't work for me.

Therapist: I'm curious what you did and for how long and how frequently?

Client: I went to the gym on a one-week free membership. I worked out twice. It didn't help and I hated it.

Therapist: Sometimes people do feel better immediately after going, but when people aren't used to exercising it might just make them tired. And you are certainly not alone in not liking the gym. I'm wondering if you'd be willing to do an experiment?

Client: I dunno. What?

Therapist: Would you be willing to walk? Ride a bike? Or go in-line skating?

Client: I'd walk.

Therapist: Makes sense. People stick to walking more than any other exercise, so you're choosing wisely. How long would you be willing to walk?

Client: Probably 30 minutes. Maybe a little longer.

Therapist: Great! How about you walk just 20–30 minutes. How many days would you be willing to do it?

Client: I don't know.

Therapist: Would you be willing to do an experiment for just two weeks and walk every other day, or more if you want?

Client: I'll try.

Motivational interviewing (Miller & Rollnick, 2012) is similar, but more involved than just using the Socratic method. It is a non-judgmental, non-confrontational, and non-adversarial approach used to motivate clients who are on the fence and can be resistant. Acceptance and commitment therapy is also aimed at resistant clients. While there is significant overlap with the concepts in this book, I recommend exploring Steven Hayes' methods when others aren't working (Hayes, 2004).

Also do experiments in the session. For example, rather than telling clients about the rationale for acceptance, try talking them through it: "Would you be willing to close your eyes? [client does so] Observing where you feel the anxiety in your body. Noticing where it's located [and so on]." Resistant clients are more likely to maintain an open mind when engaging in an experiment, than when being told what to do.

Finally, regardless of the reason for resistance, sometimes medication is the answer. Discuss with the client that medication may help them to focus and get more motivated to follow through with the strategies. Once the strategies become effective and have been maintained for several months, it may be possible to wean the client off the medication. If you can work with a physician who is willing to eventually wean a client off medication and the client knows it is likely to be temporary, they may be more willing to consider it. For clients who are resistant to medication, it may be just the thing that motivates them to start trying methods in this book.

References

Abel, J. L. (2010). *Active Relaxation: How to Increase Productivity and Achieve Balance by Decreasing Stress and Anxiety.* La Vergne, TN: Lightning Source.

Abel, J. L. (2014). *Resistant Anxiety, Worry, & Panic: 86 Practical Treatment Strategies for Clinicians.* Eau Claire, WI: PESI Publishing & Media.

Abel, J. L. (2016, February). The art of perfecting muscle relaxation: Alleviate tension, pain, fatigue, insomnia, and more [Webinar]. Retrieved May 18, 2017, from https://catalog.pesi.com/item/the-art-perfecting-muscle-relaxation-alleviate-tension-pain-fatigue-insomnia-more-13299.

Abel, J. L. & Borkovec, T. D. (1995). Generalizability of DSM-III-R generalized anxiety disorder to proposed DSM-IV criteria and cross-validation of proposed changes. *Journal of Anxiety Disorders, 9*(4), 303–313.

Abramowitz, J. & Braddock, A. (2010). *Hypochondriasis and Health Anxiety, in the series Advances in Psychotherapy, Evidence Based Practice.* Hogrefe Publishing, Boston, MA

Antony, M. M. & Swinson, R. R. (2009). *When Perfect Isn't Good Enough: Strategies for Coping with Perfectionism.* Oakland, CA: New Harbinger.

Arden, J. B. (2014). *Brain Based Therapy for OCD: A Workbook for Clinicians and Clients.* Eau Claire, WI: PESI Publishing & Media.

Asmundson, G. J. G. & Taylor, S. (2005) *It's Not All in Your Head: How Worrying about Your Health Could Be Making You Sick--and What You Can Do about It.* The Guilford Press, New York, NY.

Beck, A. T. (1967). *The Diagnosis and Management of Depression.* Philadelphia, PA: University of Pennsylvania Press.

Bernstein, D. A. & Borkovec, T. D. (1973). *Progressive Rlaxation Training: A Manual for the Helping Profession.* Champaign, IL: Research Press.

Bernstein, D. A., Borkovec, T. D., & Hazlett-Stevens, H. (2000). *New Directions in Progressive Relaxation Training: A Guidebook for Helping Professionals.* Westport, CT: Praeger.

Borkovec, T. D., Abel, J. L., & Newman H. (1995). Effects of comorbid conditions in generalized anxiety disorder. *Journal of Consulting and Clinical Psychology, 63*(3), 479–483.

Borkovec, T. D. & Costello E. (1993). Efficacy of applied relaxation and cognitive-behavioral therapy in the treatment of generalized anxiety disorder. *Journal of Consulting and Clinical Psychology, 61*(4), 611–619.

Borkovec, T. D., Newman, M. G., Pincus, A. L., & Lytle, R. (2002). A component analysis of cognitive-behavioral therapy for generalized anxiety disorder and the role of interpersonal problems. *Journal of Consulting and Clinical Psychology, 70*(2), 288–298.

Borkovec, T. D. & Roemer, L. (1995). Perceived functions of worry among generalized anxiety disorder subjects: Distraction from more emotionally distressing topics? *Journal of Behavior Therapy and Experimental Psychiatry, 26*(1), 25–30.

Brown, T. A., & Barlow, D. H. (1992). Comorbidity among anxiety disorders: Implications for treatment and DSM-IV. *Journal of Consulting and Clinical Psychology, 60*, 835–844.

Brown, T. A. Barlow, D. H., & Liebowitz, M. R. (1994). The empirical basis of generalized anxiety disorder. *American Journal of Psychiatry, 151*, 1272–1280.

Burns, D. D. (1980). *Feeling Good: The New Mood Therapy.* New York, NY: William Morrow.

Carbonell, D. A. (2014). *Panic Attacks Workbook: A Guided Program for Beating the Panic Trick.* Berkeley, CA: Ulysses Press.

Castonguay, L. G., Goldfried, M. R., Wiser, S., Raue, P. J., & Hayes, A. M. (1996). Predicting the effect of cognitive therapy for depression: A study of unique and common factors. *Journal of Consulting and Clinical Psychology, 64,* 497–504.

Dugas, M. J., Letarte, H., Rhéaume, J., Freeston, M., & Ladouceurr, R. (1995). Worry and problem-solving: Evidence of a specific relationship. *Cognitive Therapy and Research, 19*(1), 109–120.

Eifert, G. H. & Heffner, M. (2003). The effects of acceptance versus control contexts on avoidance of panic-related symptoms. *Journal of Behavior Therapy and Experimental Psychiatry, 34,* 293–312.

Ellis, A. (1975). *A New Guide to Rational Living.* Upper Saddle River, NJ: Prentice-Hall.

Grant, A. (2016, April). "The surprising habits of original thinkers" [Video]. Retrieved May 18, 2017, from https://www.ted.com/talks/adam_grant_the_surprising_habits_of_original_thinkers.

Grayson, J. (2014). *Freedom from Obsessive Compulsive Disorder: A Personalized Recovery Program for Living with Uncertainty* (updated ed.). New York, NY: Penguin Books.

Hayes, S. C. (2004). Acceptance and commitment therapy, relational frame theory, and the third wave of behavior therapy. *Behavior Therapy, 35,* 639-665.

Hayes, S. C. & Smith, S. (2005). *Get Out of Your Mind and Into Your Life: The New Acceptance and Commitment Therapy.* Oakland, CA: New Harbinger.

Houston, P. (2000). *A Little More About Me.* New York, NY: Washington Square Press.

Jakubowski, P. & Lange, A. J. (1978). *The Assertive Option: Your Rights and Responsibilities.* Champaign, IL: Research Press.

Kabat-Zinn, J. 1990. Full Catastrophe Living: Using the Wisdom of Your Body and Mind to Face Stress, Pain, and Illness. New York: New York, Random House, Inc.

Kendler, K. S., Neale, M. C., Kessler, R. C., Heath, A. C., & Eaves, L. J. (1992). Childhood parental loss and adult psychopathology in women: A twin study perspective. *Archives of General Psychiatry, 49,* 109–116.

Lee, S., Wu, J., Ma, Y. L., Tsang, A., Guo, W. J., & Sung, J. (2009). Irritable bowel syndrome is strongly associated with generalized anxiety disorder: A community study. *Alimentary Pharmacology & Therapeutics, 30*(6), 643–651.

Linehan, M. M. (1993). *Skills Training Manual for Treating Borderline Personality Disorder.* New York, NY: Guilford Press.

Llera, S. J. & Newman, M. G. (2010). Effects of worry on physiological and subjective reactivity to emotional stimuli in generalized anxiety disorder and nonanxious control participants. *Emotion, 10,* 640–650.

Miller, W. R. & Rollnick, S. (2012). *Motivational Interviewing* (3rd ed.). New York, NY: Guilford Press.

Newman, M. G. (2000). Recommendations for a cost offset model of psychotherapy allocation using generalized anxiety disorder as an example. *Journal of Consulting and Clinical Psychology, 68,* 549–555.

Newman, M. G., Castonguay, L. G., Borkovec, T. D., Fisher, A. J., Boswell, J. F., Szkodny, L. E., & Nordberg, S. S. (2011). A randomized controlled trial of cognitive-behavioral therapy for generalized anxiety disorder: With integrated techniques from emotion-focused and interpersonal therapies. *Journal of Consulting and Clinical Psychology, 79*(2), 171–181.

Newman, M. G., Castonguay, L. G., Borkovec, T. D., & Molnar, C. (2004). Integrative psychotherapy. In R. G. Heimberg, C. L. Turk, & D. S. Mennin (Eds.), *Generalized Anxiety Disorder: Advances in Research and Practice* (pp. 320–350). New York, NY: Guilford Press.

Otto, M. W. & Pollack, D. H. (2009a). *Stopping Anxiety Medication Workbook: Treatments that Work*. Oxford, UK: Oxford University Press.

Otto, M. W., & Pollack, D. H. (2009b). *Stopping Anxiety Medication Therapist Guide: Treatments that Work*. Oxford, UK: Oxford University Press.

Pleva, J. & Wade, T. D. (2007). Guided self-help versus pure self-help for perfectionism: A randomised controlled trial. *Behaviour Research and Therapy, 45*(5), 849–861.

Smith, M. J. (1985). *When I Say No, I Feel Guilty*. New York, NY: Bantam Books.

Subotnik, R., Steiner, C., & Chakraborty, B. (1999). Procrastination revisited: The constructive use of delayed response. *Creativity Research Journal, 12*(2), 151–160.

Ware, B. (2012). *The Top Five Regrets of the Dying: A Life Transformed by the Dearly Departing*. Carlsbad, CA: Hay House.

Wegner, D. (1989). *White Bears and Other Unwanted Thoughts*. New York, NY: Guilford Press.

Yerkes, R. M. & Dodson, J. D. (1908). The relation of strength of stimulus to rapidity of habit-formation. *Journal of Comparative Neurology and Psychology, 18*, 459–482.

Young, J. E., Klosko, J. S., & Weishaar, M. E. (2006). *Schema Therapy: A Practitioner's Guide*. New York, NY: Guilford Press.